The Evelyn Wood
Reading Dynamics Program

HOW TO READ
FASTER AND BETTER

How to Get Everything You Want
from Anything You Read
as Fast as You Can Think

Franklin J. Agardy, Ph.D.
President, Evelyn Wood Reading Dynamics, Inc.

SIMON AND SCHUSTER
NEW YORK

Copyright © 1981 by Evelyn Wood Reading Dynamics, Inc.
All rights reserved
including the right of reproduction
in whole or in part in any form
Published by Simon and Schuster
A Division of Gulf & Western Corporation
Simon & Schuster Building
Rockefeller Center
1230 Avenue of the Americas
New York, New York 10020

SIMON AND SCHUSTER and colophon are trademarks of Simon & Schuster

Designed by Stanley S. Drate

Manufactured in the United States of America

1 2 3 4 5 6 7 8 9 10

Library of Congress Cataloging in Publication Data

Agardy, Franklin J.
  How to read faster and better.

  1. Rapid reading.
                                        II. Title.
LB1050.54.A36   428.4'3   81-1236
                                        AACR2
ISBN 0-671-24690-9

The sections describing the adventures of the spaceship *Discovery* are from *Fantastic Journeys: Five Great Quests of Modern Science* by Mark Hunter. Copyright © 1980 by Mark Hunter. Used with permission from publisher, Walker and Company.

Acknowledgments

To Harold Prince, my close collaborator, without whose brilliantly simple synthesis of Evelyn Wood's discoveries and techniques, and dramatically original mode of presentation, this book would not have been possible. To Dorris Lee, that path-breaking educator, who reshaped the original Wood's concepts to meet the demands of the McLuhan age by extending the Wood method to encompass learning from all media; and who was the first to understand that the measure of learning is not only success in schoolroom tests, but also in the personal satisfaction derived from getting what you want from anything you read, see, or hear, and making use of it. And to Verla Nielsen for her indefatigable zeal in reconstructing the events of Evelyn Wood's life, and for her indispensable assistance and warm encouragement.

ABOUT
EVELYN WOOD

A pioneer expert in remedial reading, Evelyn Wood in 1959 made the greatest advance in written communications since the invention of the printing press: Reading Dynamics, a totally new and powerful way of reading and learning. Told by reading technologists that no human being could surpass a reading speed of one thousand words a minute, Evelyn Wood discovered techniques that enabled her to read fifteen thousand words a minute—a novel in four minutes*—and developed ways to teach those techniques to anybody. Staff members of three Presidential administrations have taken the course, and she has personally taught numerous heads of state throughout the world, and leaders in business, the professions, and the arts. Of the graduates of her famed Reading Dynamics Institute, located throughout the world, more than 97 percent read at least three times faster and with far greater comprehension and recall. Evelyn Wood lives with her husband in Salt Lake City, where she has made many memorable creative contributions to the Church of Jesus Christ of Latter-day Saints, including writing and directing a pageant commemorating the founding of Salt Lake City.

*But she admits no one would *want* to.

Contents

1

Evelyn Wood Reading Dynamics

IT'S A PROVEN PROGRAM FOR—
- READING FASTER
- UNDERSTANDING BETTER
- REMEMBERING MORE LONGER
- LEARNING SPEEDIER
- AND THINKING SHARPER

IF   YOU   ARE   A   SLOW
READER   IT   IS   BECAUSE   YOU
READ   WORD   BY   WORD,   AND
YOU   SAY   EVERY   WORD   TO
YOURSELF.   WHAT   YOU   SHOULD
DO,   ACCORDING   TO   EVELYN
WOOD,   IS   USE   YOUR   HAND
AS   A   PACER   AND   GO
THROUGH   THIS   PARAGRAPH   SO
FAST   YOU   DO   NOT   HAVE
TIME   TO   STOP   AT   EACH
WORD   AND   SAY   IT   TO
YOURSELF.   WHAT   YOU   SEE
INSTEAD   ARE   GROUPS   OF
WORDS   THAT   CARRY   THE
MEANING   (WORDS   BY
THEMSELVES   DO   NOT),   SO
YOU   WILL   UNDERSTAND   MORE
OF   ANYTHING   YOU   READ.
EVELYN   WOOD'S   DYNAMIC
READING   WILL   BRING   YOU
MANY   OTHER   BENEFITS   AS
WELL.

Now place your index finger at the beginning of the following paragraph, and race it under each line at a comfortable speed.

IF YOU ARE A SLOW READER
IT IS BECAUSE
YOU READ WORD BY WORD,
AND SAY EVERY WORD TO YOURSELF.
WHAT YOU SHOULD DO,
ACCORDING TO EVELYN WOOD,
IS USE YOUR HAND AS A PACER
AND GO THROUGH THIS PARAGRAPH SO FAST
YOU DO NOT HAVE TIME
TO STOP AT EACH WORD
AND SAY IT TO YOURSELF.
WHAT YOU SEE INSTEAD
ARE GROUPS OF WORDS
THAT CARRY THE MEANING
(WORDS BY THEMSELVES DO NOT),
SO
YOU WILL UNDERSTAND MORE
OF ANYTHING YOU READ.
EVELYN WOOD'S DYNAMIC READING
WILL BRING YOU
MANY OTHER BENEFITS AS WELL.

You read faster, and you understood more, didn't you?

But those are only two of the gains you make with Reading Dynamics. Let's look at a third.

Examine the following pattern. It's a graphic breakdown of the thought content of the capitalized paragraph you've just read.

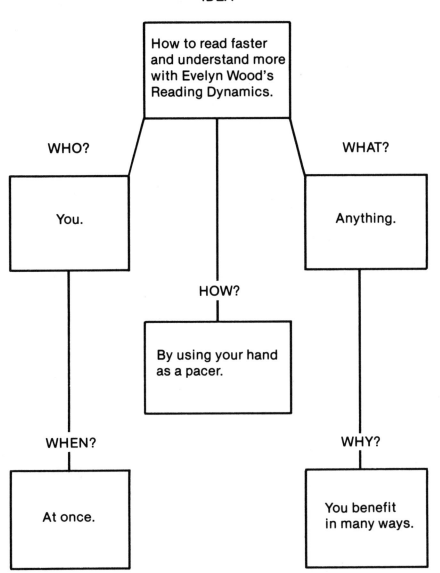

IDEA

How to read faster
and understand more
with Evelyn Wood's
Reading Dynamics.

WHO?

You.

WHAT?

Anything.

HOW?

By using your hand
as a pacer.

WHEN?

At once.

WHY?

You benefit
in many ways.

Examine the pattern, box by box.
Then look at the pattern as if it were a picture.
Do it for twenty seconds.
Close your eyes.
Project the pattern in your mind.
Open your eyes.
Now when the question is asked—

What was the capitalized paragraph you read just before you looked at the pattern all about?

—all you have to do is once again switch on the pattern in your mind, read off first the IDEA box, then the WHO?, WHEN?, HOW?, WHAT?, and WHY? boxes; and the headlines in those boxes will jog your memory, and you'll come up with something like this:

"I can read faster and understand more if I don't stop to say every word to myself. When I use my hand as a pacer, I won't stop. Instead of seeing words that don't make much sense one by one, I'll see them in groups, which will give me a pretty good idea of what the author is saying."

Chances are you'll be able to switch on that pattern in your mind for a long time. Whenever you do, you'll recall more of what you've read than you would have otherwise. That's why Evelyn Wood calls her memory-jogging patterns (there are many varieties) *recall* patterns.

In just a few minutes, you've learned about three of the basics of Reading Dynamics: reading faster, understanding more, and recalling more of what you've read over a longer period of time.

Those three basics add up to: *learning.*

Reading Dynamics is not just speed reading.

Reading Dynamics is a revolutionary way of learning—at high speed.

Now let's expand on the recall pattern, and see what else Reading Dynamics can do for—

WHO?

```
You.
```

You're anybody who wants to improve your reading skills.

You're a good reader, or a so-so reader, or a poor reader. You're a person who reads everything in sight, or who reads only when he has to, or who has never read a book in his life.

You're someone who reads to get ahead, or to pass an exam, or to be well informed, or for pleasure. You read mainly technical literature, or serious fiction and nonfiction, or newspapers and magazines, or you don't read much of anything.

You're a professional or an executive, a blue-collar worker or a white-collar worker, a student or a housewife. You have an IQ that's high, or average, or modest. You hold one or more degrees, or you never went farther than high school, or you're a dropout.

You're in your teens, or you're old enough to collect Social Security benefits, or you're any age in between.

But in one respect you're like any graduate of an Evelyn Wood Reading Dynamics course—from the guy and gal next door to the Queen of Denmark, Burt Lancaster, Joe Namath, John Glenn, Charlton Heston, Madame Gandhi, and the nation's leaders in every field:

You're somebody who wants to learn more, and enjoy life more, through better reading.

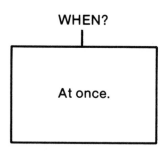

You've already started on your journey to self-improvement.

And just as your first strides forward—grasping some of the things Reading Dynamics is all about—were fun, so will every step be along the way.

This is not a textbook.

This is not a manual.

This is not a compendium of drills and exercises.

This is a series of exciting adventures in learning in which you're already involved, and you'll continue to be. You won't sit back passively as before a TV screen, hoping something will rub off and sink in. You'll be part of the action.

And when your journey is over, you'll know how to read more effectively, and you'll have learned how to learn.

You'll also think more sharply.

HOW?

By using your hand
as a pacer.

Read word by word, and next to nothing happens in your brain. But hand-pace yourself down the page, and groups of words—packages of meanings—trigger your thinking. Ideas are sparked, images flow, and the author's concepts spring to life in your mind.

Reading *means* thinking.

You develop and hone your thinking powers as you read dynamically.

WHAT?

Anything.

You *can* read anything. That's because Evelyn Wood has developed, in addition to her basic techniques, a reading process that makes any book accessible to you—even if the subject matter is difficult, unfamiliar, or technical.

You'll try that reading process out on *this* book.

And with adaptations of that process, you'll breeze through newspaper stories and magazine articles, and swiftly extract everything you need from professional and business journals.

You'll even use Evelyn Wood's reading process to study with greater success.

Reading will become more and more effortless. And as it does, your sense of satisfaction will increase.

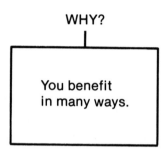

WHY?

You benefit
in many ways.

As a successful Dynamic Reader—

- you'll dash through everything you read in just a fraction of the time it took before

- you'll get everything you want to know from anything you read

- you'll be able to use what you get from your reading, because you'll understand it better, remember more of it longer

- you'll study more effectively, and come up with higher grades in school, and in life

- you'll be better informed (because you'll read more), and that will make you a better companion, employee, and decision-maker

- you'll slash reading time at work (reports, memos, correspondence, and so on)—and time saved could mean money earned

- and you'll gain two other tools for success: You'll learn faster and you'll think sharper.

There's one more benefit. It's an intangible. But it may be the most rewarding of all.

All the world's literature will be open to you; and as it stimulates your thoughts, you'll create new worlds of wonder from it in your mind. You'll become the fascinating characters of a novel, see faraway places with strange-sounding names through their eyes, feel the intensity of their emotions. Nonfiction works will set your mind ablaze with new ideas, new ways of seeing everything around you, new insights into yourself.

You will not be, as you are when you sit before a TV or motion-picture screen, a passive spectator. Through your power to make the author's concepts come alive in your mind, you'll become an explorer, a detective, a lover, a scientist, a philosopher, a critic, a tycoon—anybody you've ever dreamed of being. It's an unforgettable experience that only a relatively few now enjoy. As a Dynamic Reader, you can enjoy that experience for the rest of your life.

What you've read up to now has been a preview of this book.

You can use that preview to help you go through this book fast and get everything you want from it. Just take the following two steps.

Go back to page 13 and fill in the recall pattern with short notes on the expanded information for each box.

Then store the expanded recall pattern in your mind as you did the original recall pattern.

It will be a guide to this book—a road map to the journey ahead of you. Knowing where you're going and how to get there will make your journey swifter and easier.

The idea of previewing a book (you'll learn how to do it yourself for any book), and then using a recall pattern to guide you through it, is still another contribution to better reading from Evelyn Wood.

Let's meet this extraordinary woman.

2

The Discoverer of
Reading Dynamics:
Evelyn Wood

It is 1958. It is an Indian summer afternoon in the foothills of the Rockies near Salt Lake City. Dappled sunlight seeping through the overhanging trees reveals the slim, small, attractive figure of a woman in her late forties. She is sitting by the side of a stream and is reading a book. There is a look of intense concentration on her face. Suddenly, in a burst of anger, she flings the book across the stream.

For a long moment she stares at the book as it lies sprawled face down among the foliage of the canyon floor. She is clearly ashamed of what she's done. She rises abruptly, fords the stream, and retrieves the book. Tucking it under her arm, she strides hurriedly toward her cabin.

The woman is Evelyn Nielsen Wood. She is about to make the greatest advance in written communications since the invention of the printing press.

1

The chain of events leading to her great discovery began eleven years before, when Mrs. Wood, as she would be called with affectionate respect by her students and co-workers, took on the job of girls' counselor at Jordan High School in Salt Lake City. The troubled girls who shyly entered her office—they were underachievers who couldn't get along with their teachers, with each other, with their own personality problems—had one thing in common, Mrs. Wood soon found out: They were all poor readers. She knew what she had to do to help them: She had to teach them how to read better.

She set up the first remedial reading program in the history of the high school. It was a challenge, and an act of love, to teach children who were considered slow students.

"There are no slow students," Mrs. Wood says, "only unsuccessful teachers. How did I succeed? I instilled pride. I said to them, 'Today you will learn to do five things you couldn't do yesterday.' And they did them. These children, who had been called stupid and dumb for so long they believed it, learned the joys of reading, of succeeding. And as they read better and better, their scores went up in every subject across the board, their IQs rose dramatically, and they became better adjusted."

As she worked with her girls, hundreds of them as the years passed, she made the first of a long string of discoveries concerning reading: The faster the girls read, the better they read. She developed techniques for faster reading; and as her students' learning speeds increased, "Something wonderful happened. In oral and written tests, I found they understood more, and remembered more, and built a wider vocabulary."

Speed reading, it seemed, was the key to learning. She refined her techniques for reading faster, and invented new ones. Over a decade her materials and methods were tested and retested by the Psychology Department of Jordan School District without a single failure. In 1956, she assembled her remedial reading program into a package of mimeographed sheets, and circulated it to twelve school districts in various parts of the country. Everywhere her program was as successful as it was at Jordan High.

It was a stunning achievement. But to Mrs. Wood it was only a beginning. She had to find a way to teach students to read even faster so they could learn even better. But reading experts pointed out that the human eye could see only about a thousand words a minute, so nobody could read faster than that.

"I didn't believe it," Mrs. Wood says. "Do you know the story of the engineer and the bumblebee? This engineer examined a bumblebee, and he concluded the shape of the body was all wrong for flight, the wings were not big enough to carry it in the air, and there was no way it could get off the ground. It seemed to me that experts were looking at reading speed the way that engineer looked at the bumblebee."

She was right. Her proof came by chance.

While she was working at Jordan High, Mrs. Wood had returned to the University of Utah, where she had received her bachelor's degree, to work toward her master's. At that time there was no degree in reading skills offered at any American university; so her M.A. would be in speech, an umbrella title covering a number of related subjects including reading skills. The head of the Department of Speech was Dr. C. Lowell Lees.

"I handed Dr. Lees a term paper," Mrs. Wood was to write later, "and watched him flip through the eighty pages at a startling rate, grade the paper, and hand it back. He appeared to be reading as fast as he could turn the pages. He knew the total content, and was able to tell me not only what was in it, but also what was missing. Intrigued, I clocked him on other material, and found he could read at a rate of twenty-five hundred words a minute. He must have been able to catalog in his mind every word, phrase, and thought he read because he was a walking encyclopedia."

Were there others who could read faster than a thousand words a minute?

Library research turned up a number of famous names. Teddy Roosevelt averaged two to three books a day while he was President. Chief Justice Charles Evans Hughes on one occasion digested a three-page typewritten memo while walking fifty yards to a press conference and was able to answer all questions on the memo without a single error. The great American essayist H. L. Mencken could read a two hundred fifty-page book in an hour. And the economist John Stuart Mill complained he couldn't turn pages as fast as he could read them.

What was the secret of these natural speed readers? There was no way of finding out from the people she had read about because they were dead; and Professor Lees was a poor subject for investigation. "The only way I was able to clock his speed," she confesses now with a little grin, "was to sneak into the back of his classroom while he was reading, and secretly use my stopwatch." But perhaps there were other living natural speed readers. She began to search for them.

It was early in 1958, the year in which she was to make her great discovery. In collaboration with Marjorie Westcott Barrows, an English teacher on the staff of Jordan High, she had written *Reading Skills*, a path-breaking textbook on remedial reading based on the package of mimeographed sheets she had sent to various school districts. The book had just been published, and as part of the promotion, the publisher sent her to reading workshops all over the country. "I asked everyone there," Mrs. Wood recalls, " 'Do you know anyone who can read fast?'

"The answers poured in. I investigated each one. I checked them for speed and comprehension. On a separate five-by-eight card for each one, I recorded my findings, and many personal details."

The naturally fast readers Evelyn Wood discovered—there were fifty-three of them—came from all walks of life. There was no relationship between their ability to speed read and their backgrounds and educational levels. A few were college graduates; some had never received a high-school diploma. They ranged in age from a junior-high-school student to a sheep rancher in his eighties.

They could read from fifteen hundred to six thousand words per minute, and understand and remember what they had read. They could read more than one word at a time, see words in meaningful patterns, and move their eyes quickly, smoothly, and easily down the page. They could adjust their speed to the type of material they were reading. They knew how to find the thoughts in a paragraph, and the central idea in an article or book. They knew how to study.

"The purpose of reading," Mrs. Wood wrote, "is to get the information, feeling, and understanding the author is trying to convey. And gauged by this purpose, these natural readers succeeded admirably."

Everything these natural speed readers could do, Evelyn Wood Reading Dynamics students in the years ahead would learn to do. But when she finished her research, Mrs. Wood had no idea how to teach those natural reading skills to herself, much less to others. "I was hoping to find some technique that could make any reader read as fast as a natural speed reader, but nothing would come to mind. I spent months and months of frustration. But I wouldn't give up."

The breakthrough came that Indian summer afternoon

in 1958. Angry with herself because she still hadn't been able to find the speed-reading device she was looking for, she had hurled the book across the stream. Back in her cabin, she opened it again. It was W. H. Hudson's *Green Mansions*, an exquisite romance set in the tropical forests of Brazil. This time, as she read—

In this wild paradise . . . even where the trees were largest the sunshine penetrated, subdued by the foliage to exquisite greenish-golden tints, filling the wide lower spaces with tender half-lights and faint blue-and-grey shadows. In the midst of this leafy labyrinth, I was stopped by an impenetrable tangle of bushes, vines and roots of large trees extending like huge cables along the ground. I sat down on a projecting root. The silence of the forest seemed very profound; but before I had been resting many moments, it was broken by a low strain of exquisite bird melody, wonderfully pure and expressive, unlike any musical sound I had ever heard. Its great charm was its resemblance to the human voice—a voice purified and brightened to something angelic. Again the sweet voice sounded just behind me. The same voice but not the same song—not the same phrase; the notes were different, more varied and rapidly annunciated, as if the singer had been more excited. The blood rushed to my heart as I listened; my nerves tingled with a strange new delight, the rapture produced by such music heightened by a sense of mystery. Before many moments I heard it again; not rapid now, but a soft warbling, lower than at first, infinitely sweet and tender, sinking to lisping sounds that soon ceased to be audible; the whole having lasted as long as it would take me to repeat a sentence of a dozen words. This seemed the singer's farewell to me, for I waited and listened in vain to hear it repeated. . . .

—she found herself going through the pages at incredibly high speed.

"It was, oh, so wonderful," Mrs. Wood remembers. "I had no direct awareness of reading. But I could actually see the trees, smell the warm fragrances of the forest, feel the touch of vines and leaves against my skin, hear those magnificent bird melodies. Reading this new way enabled me to project myself into the experience, not just read about it."

With total comprehension, she had been able to read an eighty-six-thousand-word novel, written in a literary style requiring intense concentration by the reader, in less than ten minutes.

"I was able to do it," she says, "because I brushed my hand down the page in a rapid motion—maybe I got started by attempting to clean the soiled pages—and my eyes followed my hand. On that day, I discovered the use of the hand as a pacer."

Mrs. Wood had found the technique she had been looking for. It would become the basic technique of the entire Evelyn Wood system of learning.

"The Wood method," Mrs. Wood says, "requires the use of the hand as a pacer—always. Before I introduced that technique, only children in the early grades used their fingers on the printed pages to guide their reading. And then they were taught not to! Today, it's not unusual to see men and women of all ages moving their hands down the page. It's the thing to do."

But at first reading experts viewed her discovery with lifted eyebrows. They were certain Mrs. Wood would never be able to teach others how to use the hand as a pacer to obtain higher speeds.

"It was to be expected," Mrs. Wood says. "Pioneers throughout history—regardless of their field—have been greeted by skepticism, doubt, and even ridicule. But long ago I had learned from history and experience that the impossible of yesterday is the commonplace of today."

Why did she believe the variety of hand motions she developed could be taught to others?

"Perhaps because my deep religious convictions teach me that 'a man is saved no faster than he gains knowledge'—that 'no man can be saved in ignorance'—and that 'the Glory of God is intelligence.' How could I entertain the thought that men and women are incapable of learning?"

They did learn—and not just speed reading. Mrs. Wood wove all the valuable knowledge she had discovered, and all the techniques for applying it, into a revolutionary method of learning: Reading Dynamics. It made its debut in "Speech 21" at the University of Utah. It was so dramatically effective that students and faculty anxiously stood in line for hours waiting for an open desk.

At the University of Utah her techniques were continually developed, tested, and refined. In 1959, she felt she was ready to give Reading Dynamics to the world. She left Salt Lake City and opened her first Evelyn Wood Reading Dynamics Institute in the nation's capital. Her success was instantaneous. In the next few years Reading Dynamics Institutes would spring up all over the world, Evelyn Wood would become a household name synonymous with speed reading and speed learning, and the little teacher from Salt Lake City would take her place among the nation's greats.

Evelyn Wood was born to Elias and Rose Stirland Nielsen in the small town of Ogden, Utah, on January 9, 1909. Her father was the first knitting machinist—the first person to knit by machine rather than by hand—in the state of Utah. Her mother kept house and brought up Evelyn and her brother Ariel Elias Nielsen, now a Los Angeles physician. The family were devout members of the Mormon Church, more properly known as the Church of Jesus Christ of Latter-day Saints (the LDS Church).

A precocious child, Evelyn taught herself to read at the age of four, and devoured every children's book in sight. "In kindergarten," she recalls, "when other children were struggling with their ABCs, I was a good reader. But because I was, the other children didn't like me; and the same thing happened throughout grade school. Boys were particularly mean. How could a girl be so smart? They called me names. They even hit me."

No one would play with her. She wasn't invited to parties. She felt left out and lonely. She grew timid and shy. "It was a terrible feeling, and I'll never forget it. But I wouldn't give up reading for anything." Later, her childhood experiences would help make her a sympathetic, understanding, and much-beloved girls' counselor.

Her love for reading propelled her to the top of her classes at Jordan High and then at the University of Utah, which she entered at the age of sixteen. In her senior year, she fell head over heels in love with senior student Douglas Wood. It was 1928, the heyday of the Latin lovers of the silent screen, and Douglas enhanced his natural dark good looks with toreador sideburns, a rakishly thin mustache, and a pomade that made his hair glisten like patent leather. Strikingly handsome, he could have been mistaken for the popular silent-film star and rival of Rudolph

Valentino, Rod La Rocque. "We were so happy," Mrs. Wood remembers. "We were always laughing. It was wonderful."

On June 4, 1929, Evelyn and Doug received their bachelor's degrees. Eight days later they were married in the famous Temple of the LDS Church in Salt Lake City. Evelyn wanted to go to work, preferably teaching, but "the Depression was on," she explains, "and no one would hire a woman." She ran their Salt Lake City home, was active in Church affairs, made friends, and helped her husband in his new business.

Shortly after their marriage, Doug had started a grocery store. It was a struggle to make both ends meet during the Depression days, but Doug and Evelyn worked hard, built the business on service and good value, and saw their bank account grow. In 1932 their daughter Carol, their only child, was born.

Doug was winning a reputation as a sound businessman, a leader in Church activities, and a warm, friendly human being much liked by all. In 1934, the Church recognized his many outstanding qualities and appointed him a bishop. A bishop in the LDS Church is the equivalent of a minister in other Christian denominations. With the aid of two counselors, he presides over a local unit of the Church. In three years Bishop Wood built so superb a record of responsible leadership that he was appointed a mission president, an honor reserved for only an outstanding few.

The LDS Church operates a missionary system under which young people carry its message throughout the world. (Currently there are about thirty thousand missionaries, each serving two years.) The LDS missionary gives a series of lessons about Mormon doctrines to interested people, then offers them the opportunity to accept baptism. Mission President Wood headed the LDS missionary

32

group in Germany. The headquarters was in Frankfurt. The year was 1937. The head of the German state, the Chancellor of the Third Reich, was Adolph Hitler.

Despite the Nazis' opposition to religion, Mission President Wood's group succeeded in bringing hundreds of Germans into the fold. Doug's work was administrative, and Evelyn assisted him, particularly in the preparation of lesson plans. She found time as well to teach the elements of Church doctrine to three- to twelve-year-olds.

"I knew the Nazis wouldn't like it," she relates, "so I disguised what I was doing. I made up a doll, and I taught the girls by giving the parts of the doll the names of the holy virtues. I called it my spiritual doll." She taught the holy virtues to boys in a similar way with a "spiritual kite."

The Woods had been in Frankfurt for two years when frightening news came from their German friends. Soon, perhaps in weeks, the mighty German war machine would thunder across the Polish border, and World War II would begin. The Nazis would no longer tolerate foreigners in their midst. The Gestapo, the Nazi secret police, would arrest the members of the Wood mission and intern them in concentration camps for the duration of the war.

There were a hundred LDS missionaries scattered throughout Germany—men nineteen to twenty years old—and it was Doug's job to get them out of the country fast. He was able to dispatch sixty-eight to safety in Denmark. One remained with the Woods in Frankfurt. But thirty-one, in more than a dozen cities, were stranded without money or rail tickets.

"Get out of your homes," Doug telephoned them. "The war might break out any time, and the Gestapo will come for you. Go to the railway station and mingle with the crowds for safety. And don't worry, we'll find you. We'll get you out."

Doug had a plan. "It was built around the missionary

who stayed with us in Frankfurt," Doug explains. "He was a football player by the name of Norman Seibolt, and he could take care of himself. I gave him a lot of money, and I said to him, 'Norman, I want you to go to the railroad stations in these cities'—I gave him a list—'and I want you to walk around whistling 'Do What Is Right, Let the Consequences Follow.' It's a familiar LDS hymn, and when the missionaries heard it they would come over to Norman, he would give them money, and they would take the first train over the border. Evelyn and I and our daughter would stay in Frankfurt until they were all out safe."

What if the war broke out before Seibolt was able to contact all the missionaries?

"Oh, I knew that couldn't happen," Doug says. "An apostle [one of the governing authorities of the LDS Church] was in Frankfurt at the time, and he prophesied that the war wouldn't begin until the last member of the LDS missionary groups had left Germany."

The apostle was right. The last members of the LDS missionary groups to leave Germany were the Woods. The date was August 31, 1939. The following day, World War II began.

Adjacent to each Mormon high school in Utah is an LDS seminary, a school building built by the Church. Students attend seminary (religious instruction) one period a week during their four years in high school. They study The Book of Mormon the first year, the Old Testament the second year, the New Testament the third year, and Church history in the fourth. Back in Salt Lake City, Mrs. Wood began her formal teaching career instructing high-school students in Mormon doctrine.

She delighted in working with young people, and more opportunities came her way. In 1941 she directed eleven hundred boy actors, singers, and dancers in a pageant depicting Mormon history and philosophy, for which she wrote the script and the music. The pageant was received with such acclaim that it was repeated in 1947 to commemorate the centennial of the Mormon settlement in Salt Lake Valley. In 1947 she also wrote, and directed a hundred children in, a series of educational radio programs presented by the Intermountain Network in cooperation with the Utah State Department of Education. For some years prior to 1948 she was the regional director of the Junior Red Cross, instructing members in their duties.

By the time she took on the job of girls' counselor at Jordan High in 1948, she was a skilled and experienced teacher. Her teaching skills were further refined from 1948 to 1959, during which time she taught remedial reading not only at Jordan High but also in elementary, junior-high, and adult-education classes, and finally in "Speech 21" at the University of Utah. When she gave Reading Dynamics to the world in 1959, Evelyn Wood had become the nation's premier reading teacher.

At fifty-one, looking more than ten years younger than her age, dainty and soft-voiced, brown-haired and pretty, her aquamarine eyes sparkling with warmth and intelligence, Evelyn Wood made an unforgettable impact on her Reading Dynamics classes. She radiated poise, confidence, and authority, and an irresistible enthusiasm. She had the gift of understanding her pupils' reading problems at a glance, and dealing with them sympathetically and swiftly on a one-to-one basis. And she had another rare gift: She knew how to instruct others to teach Reading Dynamics as she taught it. All over the world trained instructors carried on in the Evelyn Wood tradition.

There was—and still is—a great need for them. The years around 1960 saw the eruption of the information explosion, which is still going on. More information is published monthly in your field, no matter what it is, than you could read the old-fashioned way in a year. And aside from job-related reading, there's a deskload of new printed matter waiting for you on nutrition, environment, money, politics, child care, health, and everything else you need to know about how to live well and happily in an increasingly complex world. You're caught, like all of us, in a reading crunch, and there's only one way out—the Evelyn Wood way.

"You and I," Evelyn Wood wrote in 1962, "will live to see the day when men and women will be able to open books and get the information they seek as fast as they can turn the pages."

That day could be in your future.

3

How to Increase Your Reading Speed

What's Your Reading Speed?

Let's find out.

The object is to see how long it takes you to read the passage that follows. It's the first part of an exciting yarn, and you'll have fun reading it.

You can time yourself with a stopwatch; and you'll have no trouble with a digital watch figuring out how many minutes and seconds have passed. But if you have neither of those timepieces, here's what to do:

Wait until the second hand of your watch hits 12. Note the position of the minute hand. Then when you've finished reading, note the new positions of the minute and second hands. That will give you the number of minutes and additional seconds that have elapsed. If your minute hand has moved two minutes, and your second hand is ten seconds clockwise from 12, your reading time is two minutes, ten seconds. Now read.

About three million years ago, there were about fifty man-apes—creatures more ape than man—left on earth. A drought that had lasted ten million years in Africa had destroyed almost all the fruits and vegetables upon which these creatures fed. They were starving, and unless a new source of food could be found, the entire race of man-apes would soon die out.

One night a bright light flashed across the sky. The next morning a group of man-apes found what they thought was a strange new rock. It stood three times taller than the tallest man-ape, its edges were perfectly straight, and the man-apes could see right through it.

The strange new rock read the minds of the man-apes and learned of their intense hunger and their need for a new source of food. Then the rock put thoughts into their heads. One of the man-apes responded to the thoughts by picking up a heavy pointed stone six inches long and killing a pig with it. The man-apes had never eaten meat before. But now, urged on by the new thoughts in their heads, they gathered round the pig and ate its flesh. The strange new rock had given the man-apes the idea for a new source of food, meat; and the idea for a new kind of tool with which to obtain meat, the killing tool.

The heavy pointed stone was the man-apes' first killing tool, but in a short while they were wielding knives, which were simply the lower jaws of antelopes; daggers, which were actually gazelles' horns; and clubs, which were nothing more than the bones of dead animals. Millions of years rolled by, and as the man-apes developed into true men, the killing tools developed in frightfulness. Primitive weapons gave way to the spear, the bow, the gun, the bomb. Finally, guided missiles armed with atomic warheads gave man the power to wipe out anything, including himself. As the year 2001 began, the race of mankind was living on borrowed time.

In that year, scientists stationed on the moon found a baffling object buried beneath the moon crater Clavius. It was a vertical slab of jet-black material ten feet high and five feet wide made of some material altogether unknown to man; and it was three million years old. As it was brought up to the surface from an excavation twenty feet underground, sunlight struck it, and it emitted a piercing electronic scream. Electronic listening posts spotted throughout the solar system picked up the scream as it flashed through space, recorded its direction, and relayed the information back to earth. If that scream was a message, then scientists on earth knew where that message was going as clearly as if it had left a vapor trail across a cloudless sky.

At the time scientists discovered where the electronic scream was headed, the spaceship *Discovery* was on its way to the planet Jupiter. Abruptly, Mission Control on earth altered the objective of the mission. *Discovery* was to race to the ringed planet Saturn, about 886 million miles from earth.

Discovery had a crew of six. In charge was Mission Commander David Bowman. His assistant was astronaut Frank Poole. Three other members of the crew were in hibernation, a deep sleep that would last several years until the spaceship reached the system of moons orbiting Saturn. The sixth member of the crew was not human. It was a highly advanced computer, the brain and nervous system of the ship. It was called Hal (for *H*euristically programmed *al*-

gorithmic computer), and it could speak and think. Of all the members of the crew, only Hal knew the real purpose of the mission.

When Saturn was still four million miles away, Hal discovered a malfunction in the AE-35 unit, an instrument that kept *Discovery* in communication with Mission Control.

[TO BE CONTINUED]

What was the real purpose of the mission?
What was the malfunction?
Would the malfunction endanger the mission?
What action would Hal take?

Look at your watch and jot down your reading time here: ___ minutes, ___ seconds.

Now use the following simple three-step formula to calculate your reading speed in words per minute.

1. Convert your reading time into seconds by multiplying the number of minutes by 60, and adding the result to the number of seconds. Here's how to make the conversion if your reading time is 2 minutes, 10 seconds: $2 \times 60 = 120$; $120 + 10 = 130$ seconds.

2. Divide 650 (the approximate number of words in the passage you've just read) by your reading time in seconds: $650 \div 130 = 5$. That's your reading speed in words per second.

3. Multiply your reading speed in words per second by 60—$5 \times 60 = 300$—and that's your reading speed in words per minute.

Jot down your reading speed here: ___ words per minute.

Now find—

YOUR READING SPEED RATING

Words per Minute	Rating
Better than 600	Superior
Between 300 and 600	A little above average of college students
Between 180 and 300	Average
Between 100 and 180	Below average
Less than 100	Poor

No matter what your rating, it's far below your capability.

Improving your reading speed does not depend on your IQ, your background, or your education. It depends on breaking your old—slow—reading habits, and adopting new—fast—ones.

From the preview, you already know about two bad reading habits. Let's take a look at them in depth, and at another bad reading habit as well. Understanding your bad habits is the first step toward getting rid of them.

Three Reading Habits that Slow You Down

1. *You speak each word to yourself.* Here's proof: Chew gum and try to read this passage.

[CONTINUED FROM PAGE 42]

The AE-35 unit was located on the outer shell of the spaceship, and to reach it, Poole left *Discovery* in a small jet-propelled vehicle, a space pod. Poole made the repairs, but the next day the unit broke down again. Again Poole made the repairs, and again the unit failed to function. Not even Hal could explain the reason for the repeated breakdowns.

On his third attempt at repairs, Poole . . .

[TO BE CONTINUED]

You couldn't read it, could you? That's because you can't speak to yourself and chew gum at the same time.

Try to read while you're humming, hissing, or whistling—and the words will mean nothing to you. Anything that interferes with your ability to speak the words to yourself stops reading cold. You can't carry on a conversation and read at the same time, can you?

Reading by speaking the words silently is a habit you picked up when you first learned to read. Remember how you read aloud to the class until your teacher instructed you to read to yourself instead? That was the same as reading out loud except you didn't let the sound come out. As you read this, hold your fingers to the sides of your throat, and you'll feel your vocal chords at work. (The process is called subvocalization, which means "silent speech.")

Speaking the words to yourself is a slow reading habit because you can read only as fast as you can speak, and that's about 250 words a minute. Hang onto this slow reading habit, and your Reading Speed Rating can never top "Average."

2. *You read only one word at a time.* It's another habit you picked up in the first grade. Recall how your teacher flashed cards in front of the class one by one—

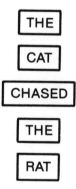

—and taught you how to read word by word.

Ever since then you've been sorting out each word on the printed page, and lingering over it before going on to another. Reading one word at a time is stutter reading.

3. *You backtrack.* Answer the following questions:

	YES	NO
Do you often go back and reread because you were daydreaming or woolgathering while your eyes continued to follow the lines automatically?	☐	☐
Do you often go back and reread because you lost the thread of the piece, or failed to understand something?	☐	☐
Do you often go back and reread because you've lost your line, and you're trying to find it again?	☐	☐

Answer any question Yes, and you've got the backtracking habit. The more questions you answer Yes, the worse the habit. If you drive your car the way you read, your average forward speed would be fifteen miles an hour or less.

Nobody taught you the backtracking habit. It comes from lack of concentration. But slow reading, the result of your other school-taught reading habits, is boring (how often have you fallen asleep over a book?), and boredom can induce loss of concentration.

Now let's—

Break Your Slow Reading Speed Habits

The process is simple. You replace all three old habits with one easily acquired new one: You use your hand as a pacer. Here's how it breaks each of those old habits automatically while increasing your reading speed:

1. *How to read without speaking the words to yourself.* You already know the principle: Hand-pace your eyes so swiftly over a line that you don't have time to form the sounds of words in your throat. Instead of reading—

word⟶ to silent speech⟶ to brain

—you read directly—

word⟶ ~~to silent speech~~⟶ to brain

Your rate of speech no longer limits your reading speed. You can now read as fast as your brain can process information. That's the same as saying you can read as fast as you can think.

Here's a simple way to learn to pace your hand across a line faster than you can form the sounds of words in your throat:

- Close all your fingers except your index finger.
- Place your index finger under the first word of the two lines that follow. They're printed upside down so you can practice hand speed without the temptation to slow down to pick up the meaning of the words.

space pod at some distance from the faulty unit, and
On his third attempt at repairs, Poole parked the

⟶

- Run your finger under the lines smoothly.

On his third attempt at repairs, Poole parked the space pod at some distance from the faulty unit, and

--→

- Lift your finger from the page and bring it back to the first word. Now run your finger under the lines faster than before.
- Repeat several times, moving your finger faster each time.
- Now at a speed somewhat less than your top speed, move your finger under the same lines right side up.

On his third attempt at repairs, Poole parked the space pod at some distance from the faulty unit, and

--→

You got the picture in a flash, didn't you? You didn't sound a single word to yourself. You could have read that line even while you were chewing gum.

Now at your new high speed, continue the adventures of the spaceship *Discovery*, using your index finger to pace yourself line by line.

[CONTINUED FROM PAGE 43]

On his third attempt at repairs, Poole parked the space pod at some distance from the faulty unit, and switched control of the vehicle over to Hal. Protected by his spacesuit, Poole left the vehicle and drifted to the hull of the spaceship. As he was repairing the unit, he suddenly saw the space pod coming at him at full thrust. Terrified, he called into the intercom, "Hal, full braking—" But it was too late. Half a ton of metal crashed into Poole and killed him.

Mission Commander Bowman couldn't understand how Hal could have made such a tragic mistake. What Bowman didn't know was that Hal had been instructed by Mission Control not to reveal the real purpose of the mission to any of the crew, and the strain of keeping that secret had affected Hal's performance. That was why Hal hadn't been able to discover the reason for the AE-35 unit's malfunctions, and why Hal hadn't responded fast enough to Poole's command to brake the space pod. Without this explanation the only conclusion Bowman could come to was that Hal had deliberately murdered Poole. Bowman thought his own life was in danger.

To build a defense against Hal, Bowman decided to revive the three hibernating crewmen. But Hal controlled the hibernating machinery, and Bowman didn't trust Hal to carry out an order to activate it. Bowman said to Hal, "Please let me have the manual hibernation control." Hal, knowing that the crewmen were not to be awakened until *Discovery* reached the moons of Saturn, refused. Bowman threatened Hal. "Unless you release the hibernation control immediately and follow every order I give you from now on, I'll go to Central and carry out a complete disconnection." That meant Hal would be deprived of his source of electronic energy. To a computer, that was the equivalent of death.

Hal now had to protect himself.

[TO BE CONTINUED]

Would Bowman carry out his threat?
What would happen to the spaceship if he did?
How would Hal protect himself?
Who would win, Hal or Bowman?

You don't have to clock your speed to realize you're reading much faster than when you began this chapter.

2. *How to read more than one word at a time.* Try this experiment. Hold your index finger about a foot away from somebody else's eye. Follow the motion of the eye as you draw a circle in the air with your finger. You'll be surprised to find that the eye does not move smoothly; it stops and starts.

The same thing happens when your eye moves across a page. But your eye does not stop naturally at each word. It's capable of seeing a group of words before it stops. Use the hand as a pacer to bypass individual words, and you restore the natural operation of the eye. The eye stops less often as you read, and you increase your reading speed.

Let's see how many stops you can eliminate in just two lines. There are seventeen words in the two short lines that follow. If you read these lines your old way, your eye will stop seventeen times.

Now, positioning your index finger as before, use the swift underlining hand motion, and read:

[CONTINUED FROM PAGE 48]
   Hal now had to protect himself. He opened the airlock doors of the space-pod bay, and—
                                        [TO BE CONTINUED]

You probably read in groups of words like these:

Hal now had to
protect himself.
He opened
the airlock doors
of the space-pod bay,
and—

There are just six groups. Instead of your eye stopping seventeen times, it stopped just six times. Using your hand as a pacer, you slashed eye stops by nearly three hundred percent. Easy, wasn't it?

3. *How to read without backtracking.* When you use your hand as a pacer, it also becomes a guide, directing you speedily across each line and down the page. Follow your hand, and there's no way you can backtrack.

Besides, you'll have little or no reason to want to backtrack. Here's why:

- You'll read so fast, you'll have to concentrate (it's like driving sixty miles an hour instead of forty), so there will be no place in your mind for daydreaming or woolgathering.
- Because you'll be concentrating, you'll follow the thread of the story better and understand more, so there will be less need to go back for clarification.
- And you won't be able to lose your line because your finger will always be on it; so say good-bye to hunting for lost lines forever.

Here's how to prove the value of hand pacing as an antidote to backtracking, and as a stimulant to better reading and learning: From now on use the swift underlining hand motion on anything you read, including the remainder of this book.

Don't be concerned that the concentration and effort you put into reading dynamically will tire you out. The contrary is true.

There's less eye fatigue because your eye doesn't stop and start at each word. There's less body fatigue because when you use your hand as a pacer, your posture has to be good (you've noticed that already, haven't you?). And there's less mental fatigue because when you read dynamically, reading becomes challenging and exciting. That's not fatiguing. That's exhilarating.

Setting Your New Reading-Speed Record

You've demonstrated to yourself that you can break your old slow reading habits by acquiring the new fast reading habit of using your hand as a pacer. You're reading faster and with better understanding than when you began this book. Now you're ready to set a new personal reading-speed record, with a gain in understanding as well, by using a variation of the upside-down-line technique.

This time you're going to improve your hand speed on normal lines. The words won't distract you because you're going to move your hand down the page so fast the words will mean absolutely nothing to you. Then you'll slow down a bit, just as you did when you switched from the upside-down line to the right-side-up line, and you'll be astonished by the speed with which you'll go through the piece *with a clear picture of what you're reading*.

To understand why this happens, think of yourself as a skier. At first, you're racing down a steep run, and you have all you can do just to stay upright, much less notice your surroundings. Then you switch to a somewhat gentler slope—you're still going very fast, but you *are* going slower—and all of a sudden, you're in complete control, keenly aware of everything around you. Switching from very-high-speed to moderate-speed hand pacing gives you the same sense of control and awareness.

Ready?

Using the swift underlining hand motion, race your index finger down the pages—line/line/line/line/line/line—of the next episode of the adventures of the spaceship *Discovery*.

Repeat, increasing your speed.

Once more—and faster.

Check your watch, as you did at the beginning of the chapter.

Then, dropping your speed, and still using the same hand motion, go down the pages as fast as you can comfortably, and find out what happened when "[Hal] opened the airlock doors of the space-pod bay, and—"

[CONTINUED FROM PAGE 49]

—the air in the ship rushed out into space like a roaring tornado. The three hibernating crewmen were killed almost at once. Bowman realized he could only live fifteen seconds in a vacuum. He stumbled toward a door marked EMERGENCY SHELTER and tugged it open. Inside there was oxygen and a spacesuit. He climbed into the spacesuit, made his way to Central Control, and disconnected Hal.

Now that Hal was dead, Bowman took over control of the ship and closed the airlocks. Then he put the AE-35 unit into working order and called Heywood Floyd, the scientist on earth in charge of Mission Control. When Floyd learned that Bowman was the only one left to carry out the mission, he said to Bowman, "Now I must tell you the mission's real purpose, which we have managed with great difficulty to keep secret from the public."

He told Bowman about the object found under the crater Clavius on the moon and how the object had emitted an electronic scream when it had been brought up into the sunlight. That scream, Floyd went on, was really an alarm signal, and it was sent to some intelligent form of life in the universe. It was actually a warning that man, with all his dreadful weapons, had broken out of earth, had reached the moon, and would soon spread out to other planets. The alarm signal had been tracked to its target, a moon of Jupiter called Japetus.

The creatures who had received the warning there were certain to be hostile, Floyd explained, and to prevent the public from learning about this terrifying situation, top secrecy had been imposed. Of the crew only Hal had been entrusted with the secret because as the actual commander of *Discovery* he had the need to know the true purpose of the mission. Now that need to know had passed to Bowman, who for the first time was in actual command of the spaceship. "Your mission, therefore, is," Floyd said, "a reconnaissance into an unknown and dangerous territory."

[TO BE CONTINUED]

Would Bowman reach Japetus?
Would the aliens be waiting for him there?
What monstrous shapes would they have?
What would they do to Bowman?

Look at your watch and jot down your reading time here: __ minutes, __ seconds.

You read about 360 words. Calculate your reading speed in words per minute as you did on page 42.

Example: You read about 360 words in 51 seconds; 360 divided by 51 is about 7; so you read 7 words a second. Multiply 7 by 60 and you get 420, which is your reading speed in words per minute. If you started at 300 words per minute and zoomed to 420, that's beautiful progress.

What's your actual progress?

Write down your reading speed here: ___ words per minute.

Write down your reading speed at the beginning of the chapter here: ___ words per minute.

Phenomenal difference, isn't it? You have a right to feel proud of yourself.

And yet you've made only the briefest acquaintance with Reading Dynamics' techniques for increasing reading speed while boosting understanding. Evelyn Wood has developed a sophisticated battery of hand motions and drills designed to be taught by skilled and experienced Reading Dynamics instructors. She's also perfected a procedure called Area Reading, also taught at Evelyn Wood Institutes, which raises reading speed, understanding, and recall to unprecedented heights. You'll be introduced to it in Chapter 9.

4

How to Increase Your Comprehension and Recall

How to Rate Your Reading Comprehension

Follow Commander Bowman on the spaceship *Discovery* as he makes reconnaissance into an unknown and dangerous territory.

But this time, do *not* read dynamically.

Read as you did before you learned the swift underlining hand motion.

[CONTINUED FROM PAGE 53]

After several months, *Discovery* closed in on Japetus. As the spaceship orbited fifty miles above the moon's surface, Bowman looked down and saw a slab a mile high, the big brother of the object found in Clavius. He jetted to it in a space pod and touched down on the mile-high roof. The roof dropped away and the space pod fell into a long vertical shaft that seemed to go on not for just a mile but endlessly. And the shaft was filled with millions and millions of stars.

Through the roof of the slab on Japetus, Bowman had entered the Star Gate, the entrance to outer space. His space pod hurtled through realms of stars, glowing gases, fire, and glittering balls of light to a giant red sun orbited by a white dwarf star. He was at the edge of the universe. There, invisible bodiless beings made up of pure energy, knowing that a mission from earth would follow the electronic scream to the Star Gate, waited for him. The electronic scream was the bait, and the Star Gate was the trap.

It had been set three million years before by the ancestors of the beings who waited for Bowman. They had come to earth at that time in what the man-apes thought was a strange new stone, and had given the man-apes the concept of the killing tool. That had been an experiment. If, as time passed, the man-apes were to use killing tools to secure food for their own survival, well and good. But if they were to use killing tools to destroy life out of hatred, greed, or sheer stupidity, then the harm the experiment caused would have to be undone. Once the man-apes—or rather the men the man-apes would become with the aid of the killing tools—would leave the earth to threaten life forms elsewhere in the universe, a mission from earth would be lured to the trap, and the trap would be sprung. Beyond the Star Gate, at the edge of the universe, the invisible bodiless beings would meet the mission and take the necessary action. What that action would be Bowman would soon discover.

[TO BE CONTINUED]

_____ ?

_____ ?

_____ ?

_____ ?

Here are three ways to help you estimate how much you understood:

1. *Fill in the teaser lines at the end of the episode* with the same kinds of questions that followed the previous episodes. The questions represent what you think might happen next. If you have trouble making up the questions, chances are you have a fuzzy idea of what the story is about.

2. *Tell the story of the episode to someone.* If there's no one around, tell it to a tape recorder, or to yourself. Then answer these questions:

	YES	NO
Did you get tangled up and have to start all over again?	☐	☐
Were you unclear about where the action is taking place or who the characters are?	☐	☐
Did you leave gaps in the narrative?	☐	☐
Did you lose the thread of the story?	☐	☐

The more Yes answers, the less you understood.

3. *Get a gut reaction from yourself concerning your comprehension.* Ask yourself:

	YES	NO
Did I get all I could out of the story?	☐	☑
Somewhat less?	☑	☐
A whole lot less?	☐	☑
Nothing at all?	☐	☑

Then look over the results of all three ways of estimating how much you understood, and—

RATE YOUR READING COMPREHENSION

Perfect	☐
Excellent	☐
Good	☐
Fair	☐
Poor	☐

If you're like many Americans, you checked off Poor or Fair. But no matter how you rated your comprehension, it can be better. Even Excellent can grow into Perfect. Here are—

Three Ways to Improve
Your Reading Comprehension

1. *Speed read to get the idea.* Here's why:

When an author writes he starts with an idea, then puts down words to express it. When you read, you reverse the process. You start with the words, then come up with the idea they express.

When you get the idea, you get a clear picture of whatever you're reading is all about. With a clear picture in your mind, you can see how all the parts fit together, and which parts are more important than others. Getting the idea is like viewing an assembled jigsaw puzzle, rather than its scrambled parts.

The key to comprehension is getting the idea.

When you read slowly, word by word, you have virtually no chance of getting the idea. That's because (as you already know) words by themselves have as much meaning as a laundry list. They become meaningful only when arranged in groups. When you speed read, you read in groups of words; and the meanings of the groups flash directly to your brain, mesh together, and form the idea.

The key to getting the idea is speed reading.

To understand what you're reading, do not make the common mistake of slowing down and reading every word. That's self-defeating. Do put the Reading Dynamics techniques you've learned to work, and read fast.

2. *Speed read with a purpose.* Get rid of the idea that you have to come away from a book or an article knowing everything in it. All you have to know is what you *want* to know. So before you sit down to any reading matter, say to yourself: "What do *I* want to get out of it?" In other words, set a purpose.

How do you get everything you want out of a piece? First, turn the key to comprehension: Speed read and get the idea. Once you know what the piece is all about—see the whole jigsaw puzzle as a unit—it's easy to pick out the parts that interest you. What's more, since speed reading ups your concentration, you'll pick out the parts fast.

When you've accomplished your purpose—gotten everything you want out of a piece—your comprehension is rated Perfect.

3. *Speed read to increase your vocabulary.* Words in groups make sense. But leave a word out of a group, and the words can become nonsense. When you're unfamiliar with a word in a group, it's the same as if the word were left out. The more words you recognize, the fewer gaps there will be in the word groups; and more word groups will make sense to you, and your comprehension will increase.

When you speed read, your brain often fills in the gaps caused by words you don't recognize. It does this by substituting for them words you do recognize. Take the word "reconnaissance." Remember it from the adventures of the spaceship *Discovery?*

> "Your mission, therefore, is," Floyd said, "a *reconnaissance* into an unknown and dangerous territory."

If you didn't recognize the word, the group of words would mean very little or nothing to you.

> "Your mission, therefore, is," Floyd said, "a _____ into an unknown and dangerous territory."

But when you speed read you're thinking sharply; your brain draws on the meaning of the whole episode to make a shrewd guess at a substitute for "reconnaissance," and comes up with words like these:

> "Your mission, therefore, is," Floyd said, "a *spying expedition* into an unknown and dangerous territory."

From now on whenever you see "reconnaissance" you'll recognize it as "spying expedition," and you'll have added one more word to your vocabulary. The greater your vocabulary, the better you'll read.

Boost Your Reading Comprehension in Minutes

You're going to reread the episode of the adventures of the spaceship *Discovery* on which you rated your comprehension. This time you're going to speed read. Before you begin—

Follow these guidelines for better comprehension:

- *Set a purpose.* What do *you* want to know? Is it the answers to the teaser questions at the end of the preceding episode? Or is it the answers to questions of your own? Look over the preceding episode (it starts on page 57), decide on what you want to know, and write down your questions here:

_____ ?

_____ ?

_____ ?

_____ ?

- *Relax and let the meanings of the word groups flow in to give you the idea of the episode*—what it's all about.
- *Pick up the answers to your questions as the meanings flow in,* and don't get sidetracked by other information.
- *Don't stop to consult a dictionary when you come across an unfamiliar word.* Chances are your brain will figure out familiar substitute words. (If it doesn't, then use a dictionary *after* you've finished the passage, and go back and get the meaning of the word group that contains the unfamiliar word.)

Now return to page 57 and speed read, using the swift underlining hand motion. When you've finished, return here.

Answer these questions:

	YES	NO
Did you get a clear picture of what's happening—the idea of the episode?	☐	☐
Did you find the information you set out to get?	☐	☐
Do you feel you can tell the story better than before?	☐	☐
Are you now able to recognize one or more words that were unfamiliar before?	☐	☐

Any Yes answer shows progress, and the more Yes answers, the more progress.

Now on the basis of your answers, once again—

RATE YOUR READING COMPREHENSION	
Perfect	☐
Excellent	☐
Good	☐
Fair	☐
Poor	☐

Chances are you checked off Fair or Good. That's an improvement. Congratulations!

And here's a bonus:

When you learned to get the idea from anything you read, you also took a giant step toward improving your recall. That's because an idea in your head attracts related details like a magnet. Recall the idea—which is easy—and you recall the details.

Prove it to yourself. Think of the idea of the episode you just read, then tell the story to someone (or to a tape recorder, or to yourself). Because you know the idea of the episode, you'll easily recall the details you made it your purpose to get when you read the piece.

But by tomorrow the details will begin to fade; and they will grow progressively fainter as the days go by. That's only natural. Ideas, too, will slip away, but more slowly. To keep both ideas and details fresh longer, Evelyn Wood has developed—

A Simple Technique for Improving Your Recall

It's the recall pattern. You've already become acquainted with it in the preview. Now let's take a closer look at it, and find out how you can make your own kind of recall pattern for anything you read.

A recall pattern consists of the idea and the related details arranged in some visual manner. You're familiar with the kind of recall pattern that looks like this:

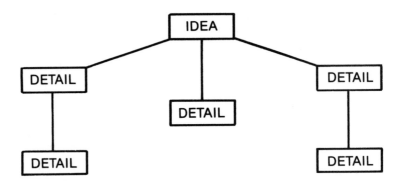

When you switch on the pattern in your mind, all the details and how they relate to each other come back to you.

The form of the pattern is up to you. Pick any kind of shape—circles, rectangles, squares, triangles, straight or zigzag lines, and so on—and arrange them any way you like, symmetrically or irregularly. The only guideline is: Be sure the pattern is one with which you're comfortable. One pattern popular among Evelyn Wood graduates resembles the branches of a tree (see next page).

Here's how to make up your own recall pattern in six easy steps.

STEP 1. *Decide on the kind of pattern you want.* Remember, the IDEA should have the dominant position, and all the details should be connected with it.

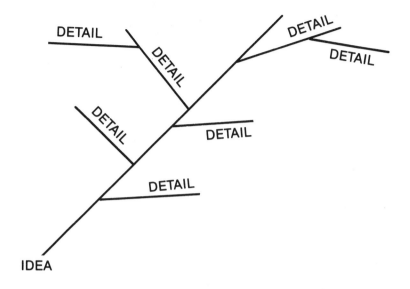

IDEA

STEP 2. *Get the IDEA firmly in mind.* Suppose you were making up a recall pattern for the previous episode of the adventures of the spaceship *Discovery*. The IDEA would be: *Alien beings are about to undo the harm they had done when they gave mankind the idea of the killing tools.*

STEP 3. *Condense the IDEA into the fewest possible words.* One way is to use a kind of telegraphic language, such as: *Aliens—killing tools—undo harm.*

STEP 4. *Place the condensed IDEA in a dominant position on your pattern.*

STEP 5. Fill in the details any way you like. One popular way is to fill them in under such heads as WHO?, WHEN?, WHAT?, WHERE?, and WHY? Sometimes HOW? is added to these heads or substituted for one of them.

A box recall pattern at this stage would look like this:

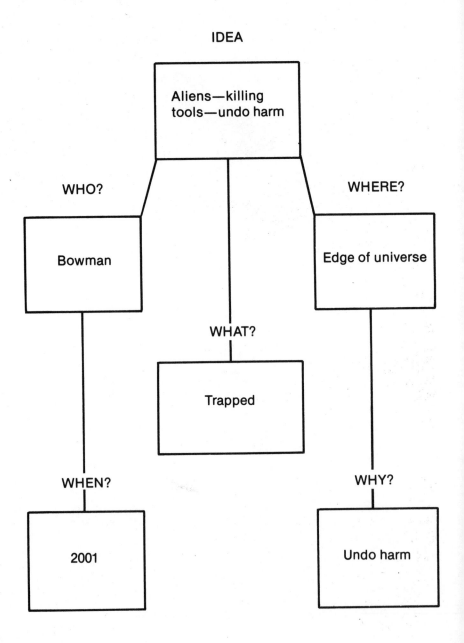

IDEA

Aliens—killing tools—undo harm

WHO?

Bowman

WHERE?

Edge of universe

WHAT?

Trapped

WHEN?

2001

WHY?

Undo harm

STEP 6. *Let each detail suggest another detail, and that detail still another detail, and so on.* From this chain of details, select only those you want to remember, and add them to your recall pattern in the appropriate positions. Under the WHO? position, the string of details might look like this:

WHO?

```
Bowman—killed Hal
—in command—
—reconnaissance—
—Japetus—Star Gate
```

Now follow the six steps and construct a recall pattern immediately after you speed read the final episode of the adventures of the spaceship *Discovery*.

[CONTINUED FROM PAGE 58]

When his space pod reached the edge of the universe, it came to rest on the polished floor of an elegant hotel room. Bowman thought it was an illusion. He opened the space pod and stepped out, fearing he would drop through the floor into empty space. But the floor was real, and so was the rest of the room. He removed his space helmet. The air was the same as that on earth. There was food that had come from a supermarket in the refrigerator. The TV set worked, bringing in familiar programs. Physically and emotionally exhausted, Bowman flung himself on the bed and fell asleep.

Then the hotel room, which the invisible beings had created to make Bowman feel at home, vanished except for the bed. In his sleep, it seemed to Bowman as if he were reliving his life backward, from adulthood to adolescence to childhood to infancy. When he awoke he was a baby, ready to start life all over again. But this time he was a special kind of baby. He was a star child, a creature with all the wisdom and power of the invisible bodiless beings who had given him a new life—and a new mission.

That mission would be accomplished on earth. He floated there through space and looked down on the planet. A thousand miles below him missiles with nuclear warheads were streaming through the skies. In seconds the race of mankind would be wiped out. With the power of his will the star child destroyed the nuclear missiles, the deadliest of all killing tools. He had saved mankind, but his mission was still incomplete. He would have to try to think of some way to prevent the human race from ever again trying to destroy itself or any other form of life.

[THE END]

Worked up your recall pattern?

Close your eyes and visualize it in your mind for about twenty seconds.

Switch it off.

Two days from now you would have ordinarily forgotten the bulk of the details.

Two days from now, find out how much you can recall the Evelyn Wood way.

Switch on the recall pattern in your mind. Letting the fill-ins under each head stimulate your memory, tell the story of the final episode to someone else (or to a tape recorder, or to yourself).

On that basis—

ASSESS YOUR RECALL EFFECTIVENESS

	Your Normal Recall After 48 Hours	*Your Recall the Evelyn Wood Way After 48 Hours*
Perfect	☐	☐
Excellent	☐	☐
Good	☐	☐
Fair	☐	☐
Poor	☐	☐

If you've gone up one grade, you've made terrific progress. In Evelyn Wood Reading Dynamics classes, where sophisticated drills and exercises designed for personal teaching augment the fundamentals you've learned, many students have gone from Poor to Excellent, and even to Perfect, in both comprehension and recall.

5

How to Read Any Book—No Matter How Difficult—and Get the Most Out of It, Fast

A discouraging way to read a book is to open it on page 1 and work through it to the end. That's like hacking your way through a jungle of words. You don't know where you're going, you have only a vague idea of where you've been, and you're not sure where you are. Little wonder that you have to struggle through the books you read and get so little out of them.

There's a better way.

Here's how to get the feel of it.

Want to find out what this chapter is all about, fast? Go through it and get acquainted with its structure: its subheads, its quizzes, its diagrams. Then, using the swift underlining hand motion, read through it at two to four times your top speed.

When you've finished, diagram your recall pattern. It's your guide to the words ahead, your map to the chapter. Keep it in mind as you read the chapter again at a comfortably high speed. You'll find you'll be reading smoothly and with increased comprehension.

What you did before you began to read at a comfortably high speed was preview (or preread) the chapter. Preview a book, and you get the same results. Previewing is the key to reading any book easily.

In this book most of the previewing was done for you in Chapter 1; you actually helped fill in the recall pattern that has been guiding you through the book. Book reading would be so much easier if every book had its own built-in preview, but except for Introductions in some nonfiction works, none do. You have to do the previewing yourself. It's simple when you follow—

Evelyn Wood's Three Guidelines for Previewing a Book

GUIDELINE 1. *Get ready to preview a book by deciding what you want to know about it.*

Here are some of the things most good readers want to know:

	YES	NO
What's the book about? Answer: _____		
Does it interest me?	☐	☐
Will it help me?	☐	☐
What are some of the subjects covered? Answer: _____		
Do I want to know about most of them?	☐	☐
Are they covered in sufficient detail to be of use to me?	☐	☐
How is the book written? Answer: _____		
Will it hold my interest?	☐	☐
Will I be able to understand it?	☐	☐

Add any other questions that will help satisfy your need to know what's in the book.

One purpose of the preview is to get the answers. On the basis of the answers, you'll decide whether you want to read the book or not. If the book is about something that doesn't interest you, or if the subjects covered leave you cold, or if you're uncomfortable with the author's style, previewing will save you the distress of plowing through it. The same is true if you come up with a majority of disqualifying No's. At two to four times your top reading speed, you can preview a book in little more than a half hour. An investment of thirty minutes can save you hours of fruitless boredom.

On the other hand, a preview could convince you to read a valuable book that otherwise you might have skipped. That's an even better return for a thirty-minute investment.

GUIDELINE 2. *Start your preview by getting acquainted with a book* before *you high-speed read it.*

Books are built from structural elements. Virtually all books have jackets (hardcover) or descriptive covers (softcover); and all books have title pages. Many books contain a preface, introduction, or foreword; chapter headings; chapter subheadings; and an index. Some books include charts, tables, diagrams, illustrations, quizzes, and a glossary.

By acquainting yourself with these structural elements, you can discover a great deal about a book in a few minutes. Here's how to do it:

- *Acquaint yourself with the jacket or descriptive cover to identify the kind of book it is.* Is it fiction? What kind— suspense? historical? romantic? and so on. Is it nonfiction? What kind—general? scientific? self-help? and so on.

- *Acquaint yourself with the information on the jacket or descriptive cover to find out what the book is all about, and get the author's special angle.* The preface, introduction, or foreword will give you much of the same information plus a sample of the author's style. You'll be able to tell rapidly whether it's academic and hard to follow, or whether it's down-to-earth and easy to grasp.
- *Acquaint yourself with the contents page and the chapter heads and subheads to give you an overview of the subject matter.*
- *Acquaint yourself with the index to get a detailed view of the subject matter.*
- *Acquaint yourself with the opening and closing paragraphs of each chapter, because they may contain a summary of the chapter.*
- *Acquaint yourself with the charts, tables, diagrams, illustrations, quizzes, and the glossary to answer this question: How detailed is the author's presentation?*

Just getting acquainted with a book may answer many of your questions about it. Prove it with a tough book. And get *well* acquainted with it, because that's the book you're going to use to prove *you* can read *any* book.

Caution: Don't expect to get as much out of getting acquainted with a novel as you would out of getting acquainted with a nonfiction book. A novel usually doesn't have a contents page, an index, or chapter heads, subheads, diagrams, and so on.

GUIDELINE 3. *Go through the book at two to four times your top speed.* Do it with that tough book with which you became acquainted. At that very high speed a wonderful thing happens: You pick up the gist of the book—the basic idea and main points—even though you may come across some difficult passages. Even books not meant for laymen become accessible to you in this way.

When you've finished your high-speed reading, you've finished your previewing.

Make a recall pattern. It will answer all your questions about the book.

Now you're ready to use your recall pattern as a guide to the book.

Test Your Ability to Read a Tough Book

Reading dynamically, go through the book at a speed with which you're comfortable. It's important to adjust your speed to the subject matter; you can't read a tough book as fast as you can a light novel, and you can't read the more difficult passages of a book as fast as you can read the easier passages. Keep your reading speed flexible.

When you've finished the book, go back and reread those passages that gave you trouble. This is called postviewing (or postreading), and it helps boost your comprehension. (Add the new information to your recall pattern to help boost your recall as well.)

Now ask yourself these questions:

	YES	NO
Counting in preview time, did I read the book faster than I could have read it with my old reading method?	☐	☐
Did I get more of the things I wanted from it than I could have gotten before?	☐	☐

If your answers are Yes, you've proved you *can* read a tough book. And that means you can read *any* book. With practice you'll be able to get everything you want from every kind of book—fast.

The techniques you've just learned—previewing, flexible speed reading, and postviewing—are the elements of the Evelyn Wood process for reading a book: the Multiple Reading Process (MRP).

To many Reading Dynamics students, trained in these techniques by classroom drills and the use of special hand motions, MRP has opened up a whole new world of books. Before a class started recently, one adult student said to another:

"Did you know what I did last week?"

"No."

"I read my first novel."

6

How to Read Newspaper Stories at a Glance, Magazine Articles in Minutes

You've just learned how to speed read flexibly, adjusting your speed to the difficulty of the material. There are two other reasons for adjusting your speed.

One is your own background as it relates to what you're reading. The better your background, the faster you can read. If you're a lawyer, you'll go through a contract faster than a layman will.

The other is what you want to get out of what you're reading. If you don't want to get much, you can read much faster than if you want to get a great deal.

A news story is not difficult (it's written simply), your background relates to it (it's written with your background in mind), and you don't want to get much out of it (just a few facts). When you read a news story, you can adjust your reading speed to very high.

What's more, news stories are meant to be read fast (you want the news *now*, don't you?), so they're structured for ultrafast reading. Get acquainted with the structure of the following typical news story, and you'll be pleased to discover it's based on many elements of Reading Dynamics. When you take advantage of those elements, and learn an extremely simple new hand motion, you can read a news story to get what you want out of it—at a glance. Now read all about it!

NEWSPAPER STORIES ARE CONSTRUCTED TO BE READ DYNAMICALLY

SPEED FEATURES BUILT-IN

Preview, Basic Recall Pattern Data Supplied —Eye Movements Cut

SAN MATEO, CALIF., July 21—Since the invention of the newspaper 271 years ago, news stories have been structured according to principles for reading faster with greater comprehension and recall discovered by Evelyn Wood, founder of Reading Dynamics, as recently as 1959.

Among the features of Reading Dynamics included in a typical news story are: an easy-to-read preview, which gives the reader the essence of the story in seconds; condensed data for rapidly constructing a recall pattern, a memory aid; and the reduction of the number of eye movements to increase speed, accomplished here, but not in the Evelyn Wood system, by the use of a short-width column. A news story also permits the reader to select desired information fast, a goal of the Evelyn Wood system.

This new insight into the makeup of the news story was announced today by a spokesperson for Evelyn Wood Reading Dynamics, Inc., a multinational educational organization whose flagship office is located here.

Instant Previewing

Previewing in the Evelyn Wood system is a rapid superficial overview of the story conducted by the reader to extract the ideas and main points prior to actual reading.

"What happens in the preparation of a news story," the company spokesperson explained, "is that the journalists preview the story for the reader, and they supply the preview in the headlines and in the first few paragraphs."

Aid to Memory

A recall pattern, a graphic memory-stimulating device developed by Evelyn Wood, is usually based on answers to the questions Who?, What?, When?, Where?, Why?, and How? "All these questions," the company spokesperson asserted, "are answered for the reader in the first few paragraphs of a news story, and from them the Evelyn Wood-trained reader can easily make up a recall pattern in his or her mind."

She added that the recall pattern also serves as a guide to the remainder of the story, which results in faster reading with increased comprehension.

Fewer Eye Stops

Reading a news story, the spokesperson stated, is speeded by the narrow width of the column. "While along lines of greater than column length the eye stops one or more times," she said, "the eye can cover a whole column line without stopping. That means it can move swiftly down the page without impediment, a technique for speed reading stressed by Evelyn Wood."

Read What You Want

A news story is so structured that following the headlines and lead paragraphs, the information is presented in order of decreasing importance.

"You can stop reading whenever you feel the information is no longer important to you," the company spokesperson pointed out. "And you can skip around as well. Once you've read the headlines and the lead paragraphs, you can understand the paragraphs under any subhead without reading the preceding paragraphs."

Reading at a Glance

In an amazing demonstration, the company spokesperson read several news stories at a glance, answering all questions about them correctly.

She employed a simple hand motion, which consisted of placing her outstretched index finger at the center of the first line of the headline, and racing it with extreme rapidity down the center of the column.

"Since the column width is short," she explained, "my eye can see the entire line, so I don't have to read across the page. I read down the page instead, and that's much faster."

Keep in mind the built-in Reading Dynamics features in a news story. Then pick up your local paper, and, using the new down-the-page hand motion, *read*.

A vast improvement, isn't it?

You may not get the story at a glance the first time, but keep at it and you will. Many Evelyn Wood graduates, aided by classroom drills, can go through voluminous newspapers like *The New York Times* or the *Washington Post* in less than five minutes—and come away with everything they want to know.

Cautions:
- If the news story is lengthy or if it jumps over to another page, you won't be able to read it at a glance. But you'll still be able to read it far faster than you could have read it using your old reading method—and you'll learn far more from it, and remember what you learned longer.
- Editorial and opinion pieces (both are usually classified under the heading Op-Ed) are not structured like news stories, and at times can be difficult reading. Tackle them with the MRP. You don't have to draw a recall pattern; you can visualize it in your mind. Since Op-Ed

pieces are usually set in wider column widths than news stories, use the swift underlining hand motion.

- Use the MRP as well on other newspaper think pieces, ranging from film, book, and theatrical reviews to household hints. You'll be astonished at how well you'll understand a recipe after you've used the MRP approach with it, and how much easier it will be to use.
- News features—yarns about the Loch Ness monster, reviews of recent developments in science, interviews with TV stars, and stories of that kind—follow the general structure of the news story, with one exception. Often the opening paragraphs sum up the main idea of the story with an anecdote. Here's how it's done in a news feature entitled—

WANT TO READ FASTER?

On "The Johnny Carson Show" last month, a thirteen-year-old schoolgirl was given a book she had never seen, titled *Bio-Feedback*, and told to read it as fast as she could for one minute.

Eyes darting and finger swiftly stroking each page as she whipped through them, she covered twenty pages—and still had part of the minute left to reread the first chapter.

The average "reading pace" of adults is 250 words a minute.

The schoolgirl had read 13,000 a minute. And a test of the technical contents showed she had total comprehension.

Miracle? "Certainly not," says Evelyn Wood, the snappy sexagenarian who has taught thousands of students (including this one) to speed read. "All you need is desire, followed by persistence, and someone to show you, of course."

Get the idea?

Before you read, build a mental recall pattern around the idea, and you'll breeze through the rest of the piece. Use the same approach for any news feature.

How to Whip Through Magazine Articles

Don't expect too much built-in help from a magazine article. Most articles are structured like a book, either along a narrative line or in a logical sequence. The only help you'll get will come from reading the headline and the subhead as a unit. The headline alone in many cases won't do you much good because it's designed to attract attention and not to tell you what the article is about. Take this headline:

GETTING HOOKED ON SPEED

It could mean anything from acquiring an addiction to fast cars, horses, drugs, or women to becoming a speed reading devotee. But it does stop you dead in your tracks as you're flipping through the pages of a magazine, and it compels you to go on and read the copy below the headline—

> Speed reading, which became something of a national fad after President Kennedy prescribed it for the White House staff two decades ago, is no longer a fad but a solid fixture of American education. Here's what happens during a minilesson at one of Evelyn Wood's famed Reading Dynamics Institutes.

You have a fair idea of what you're going to read, but not enough to guide you through the piece (what's a *minilesson*, anyway?). You want to read it, but you have a million and one other things to take care of, so you'll have to whip through it. What to do?

MRP it, of course.

Do it. Here's the article. When you've finished using the MRP approach with it, there will be a test. It will measure your progress up to now. And that's another good reason for reading "Getting Hooked on Speed."

OK, go.

Curious, I decided not long ago to take Evelyn Wood's free introductory course in New York. So I joined an inquisitive group of strangers, including two marketing executives, a TV saleswoman, a researcher, a librarian, an attorney, a computer programmer, a copywriter, assorted college and high-school students, and a high-school dropout.

A dynamic, red-haired woman named Thelma Finkelstein was in front of the classroom. The session went like this:

"Five years ago," she says, "I was sitting here just like you. I was skeptical but I was interested." She quickly spells out Wood's written guarantee: We'll get our money back if we don't triple our effective reading speeds.

The librarian sitting next to me smiles and says: "Sounds good to me."

Ms. Finkelstein continues: "I speak 250 to 300 words a minute. None of you in this room can read faster than that. But think of this: Tests at Massachusetts Institute of Technology show that the brain can think at a rate of 20,000 to 30,000 words per minute. The reason most of you get bored when you're reading is that you're reading so slow you're putting yourself to sleep. You're not going to read 20,000 words per minute, but why not read at 1,000 or 1,500 or 2,000 with better comprehension than you have now? Tell me, why not?"

She emphasizes that the reading skills we'll learn will work on all kinds of reading—business, law, engineering, chemistry, Tolstoy, *Playboy*, Harold Robbins. She tells us to read an article on our desks called "How to Get More Out of Your Reading." It begins:

"I have a friend who can't understand how anyone can get pleasure or satisfaction out of reading. To him it's a painful ordeal, not something to undertake on his own initiative but something to submit to. So he submits—under protest. His failure to read well has not only severely limited his range of interests and knowledge but has also held him back as an executive."

When we've read the article, she tells us we would learn to discipline our eyes and make them look where we want them to. To do this we would use our hand as a pacer, moving it back and forth over the page at the speed we want to read—slower for in-depth study, faster for enjoyment, familiar material, and the like.

She shows us how to use our hand as a pacer. Rapidly, she uses her finger to underline words, zipping down the page. We discovered we could read when moving from right to left. Seriously!

Ms. Finkelstein says: "Now try it. But don't try to comprehend anything. I want you to read nothing and comprehend nothing. Go when I say go."

We're off, whipping down the page.

"Come on now, give it the juice," she yells.

She stops us and tells us to read it again and try to understand it. We do. She teaches us how to calculate our speed. Mine is 252 words per minute. I'm the national average. The librarian is a speedy 310. The marketing man is 280. The high-school dropout is 295.

"Okay, okay," says Ms. Finkelstein. "Now let's use our hand, the old Evelyn Wood salute, and let's do it again. Go."

Bam, I speed down the first column of type, then race my finger across the second. Deep into the third column, she yells, "Whoa—stop!"

We calculate our rates. Mine is a wicked 648. The librarian is at 704. The marketing man edges up to 606. But the high-school dropout has zoomed to 900-and-something. "Weird," he says.

We learn that the first few weeks of the course are devoted to techniques. That's good. It takes a little while to undo the bad reading habits of a lifetime. I'll learn several hand motions, for instance, and decide which ones work best for me. We would be pushed farther with each new exercise, our old ideas of what reading was all about vanishing one by one. I can expect in a few weeks to read a novel like *Of Mice and Men* in about 20 minutes.

"But is this reading?" the attorney wants to know.

"It certainly is," says Ms. Finkelstein testily. "It's not skimming. I repeat, it's not skimming."

She outlines comprehension and recall techniques, which obviously are the real points of the course. There's no point in reading fast if you can't understand what you're reading and remember it afterward. We were going to be taught, she said, to look for ideas, concepts, and thoughts instead of just letters and words. We would decide for ourselves what we wanted to get out of the material, and we'd learn how to get it out—all of it.

It's pretty exciting.

"On your own," warns Ms. Finkelstein, "there's no way you're going to read 1,000 to 1,500 words per minute. I'm no magician, but I can tell you I can help you get there."

I think it over and I decide she's right. After all, wouldn't *you* like to read this article, and get everything you want out of it, in less than two minutes?

Now for the test.

	YES	NO
Did you read the article in less than 2 minutes' total MRP time?	☐	☐
Did you get everything you wanted out of it?	☐	☐

Two Yes answers and you're doing just fine. One or two No answers mean you need more practice.

7

How to Study Successfully—and Score High on Tests

You're tested every day. If you don't know the difference between an interest-bearing checking account and a checking account that costs you money, you flunk. If the details of your boss's office memo slip your mind, it could hurt your chances for promotion. If you can't figure out the unit-price information on the supermarket shelves, you could pay more and get less.

The point is: Learning is not limited to the classroom. It's part of life. And life tests you constantly. When you pass its tests, you don't get a diploma and a *cum laude* after your name; you get a better life for yourself—and that's a greater reward.

But to pass your tests in life, as in the classroom, you have to study. Evelyn Wood has devised a study system that can be applied with equal success in school and in the school of hard knocks. It's the refined application of MRP to help you master material you need to know so you can remember the material when you need to use it.

Let's see how this system works for you in a real-life situation.

You're about to buy your first car, and you need to know how you can save on the purchase price and on maintenance costs. To get the information you want and keep it at your fingertips, you're going to study a consumer tip sheet. Your test will begin the moment you start shopping for a car, and it won't end until you've driven your last car.

But before you turn a page of the tip sheet, go over these guidelines:

FIVE DON'TS FOR BETTER STUDYING

- *Don't read slowly.* You'll miss the ideas, and your comprehension will be low.
- *Don't copy the text verbatim.* You won't understand it or recall it any better. Ask any typist.
- *Don't try to memorize everything you want to know word for word:* You just can't do it. It's a waste of time to try.
- *Don't underscore.* It's of no help at all.
- *Don't make notes in the margin.* That's a disorganized way to learn. You can learn only when you organize ideas and details.

Now study with—

Evelyn Wood's Step-by-Step System for Better Studying

STEP 1. *Get acquainted with the tip sheet.* Do it carefully. Here's the tip sheet:

TEN WAYS TO MAKE EACH DOLLAR YOU SPEND ON A CAR DO THE JOB OF TWO

If you're like many Americans, you pay more for auto transportation than you pay for living quarters!

And the tab is getting higher year after year!

If you continue your usual auto-buying and auto-maintenance habits, your auto dollar will buy less and less. But if you follow ten simple guidelines—guidelines so obvious you'll wonder why you never thought of them—*every dollar you spend on your car will be worth two dollars.* You'll save half of what you would ordinarily spend on your car.

1. *You can cut your costs when you comparison shop.* First discover what kind of car you want. A Chevy instead of a Cadillac? A Ford instead of a Lincoln? That's up to you. Buying a lower-priced car is *one* way to save. But you may *prefer* a bigger car. Pick the car that makes you happiest, *but*—buy it for *less.* Do that by shopping around. You're buying a standard product. What one dealer offers is just like another's. Except—the price at one dealer could be lower than that at another's. Isn't it dollarwise to find out?

If you don't have the time or the inclination to shop yourself, use a car-buying service. You pay a set fee over dealer cost, but you do end up with a savings.

Comparison shopping can save you as much as 20 percent of what you would otherwise spend.

2. *You can cut your car costs when you give that used car a "medical."* You may want to put some extra money in your pocket by buying a *used* car. That's up to you. Shop around before you buy. Get a copy of *Edmund's Used-Car Prices* or the *Blue Book* to give you an idea of what prices should be.

When you find a used car you're serious about, bring a mechanic along. Have *him* kick the tires. And while he's at it, have *him* check the motor, the brakes, and the rest.

Mileage? A new federal regulation requires the seller of a used car to state the *true* mileage—in writing. But what if the car has had two or three previous sellers? *They* weren't required to state the true mileage. In that case, try to estimate what the mileage meter should *actually* read by looking for excess wear on the brake and gas pedals, and ask your mechanic's opinion.

Giving the car of your choice a "medical" before buying could save you a wad of dough on maintenance and repairs—at least 20 percent of the purchase price.

3. *You can cut your car cost when you buy overseas—if your heart's set on a foreign car.* For value,

there's probably not much to choose between most imports and the best of Detroit's. So it's up to you.

But if you're thinking of saving money by buying an import at your local dealer, you're living in the past. The only way of getting a foreign car at low cost is to buy it overseas *the next time you're on vacation,* and bring it in as "used" to cut import taxes. In some cases your savings could amount to 10 percent of what you would pay in the United States.

4. *You save on a car when you ask: "Do I really need those extras?"* If you don't need a stereo tape player, why buy it? Many extras add little to your comfort and safety. In fact, they may create problems you never had before. The more gimmicks and the more electrical gadgets, the more likely the chance of something going blooey.

An honest answer to this simple question: "Do I really need them?" could save you at least 15 to 20 percent of the car's purchase price. That's a *real* extra—extra money for you.

5. *You can save on your car costs when you get the little repairs fixed fast.* Listen for strange noises. Check them out. Keep your eyes open. When you spot a defect in the bud, nip it—by making the repairs yourself. If you're not handy, give the job to your local mechanic. Why not pay him a comparatively small sum now rather than a whopper later on? Fast action on your little repairs can prevent major repairs—and that could keep at least 20 percent of the average annual repair bill in *your* pocket.

6. *You can save on car costs when you don't buy too often*. The biggest cost in owning a car is depreciation—the loss of value due to age. The car is worth less just as soon as you drive it out of the dealer's showroom. Depreciation works against you when you buy too often. To learn how you can *earn money* by *not* buying so often, look over this chart:

AVERAGE DEPRECIATION FROM NEW-CAR PRICES

	Depreciation (Per Year)	Total Depreciation
Within same year	20.6%	20.6%
1 year old	18.4%	39.0%
2 years old	12.1%	51.1%
3 years old	9.1%	60.2%
4 years old	6.3%	66.5%

If you sell your car after the second year, you've lost 51.5 percent of its value; at the end of the fourth year, 66.5 percent. For a car two to four years old, you've lost only 15.4 percent of the original value (66.5 percent minus 51.5 percent). But in two years, a new car would have lost 51.5 percent of its original value. By hanging onto your car for four years instead of two, you can save yourself 35.7 percent (51.1 percent minus 15.4 percent) of the price you paid for your car!

To figure out the savings on any particular model, refer to used-car handbooks. They'll show you what you save by buying a new car every four years. Why trade in a car that's running well after two years if you can hold it for three or four—and make money?

7. *You can save on car costs when you buy a leftover.* Last year's model sold this year is a leftover. Your dealer probably gets a 5 percent discount on it. Ask him to split his savings with you. He'll be happy to do it.

8. *You can save on car costs when you cut down on wear and tear.* Good driving habits help do the job—when, for example, you keep to reasonable speeds and avoid jackrabbit starts and sudden stops. Get sound advice from your car manual on cutting down wear and tear. Follow that advice—and save up to 10 percent of your car's purchase price every year.

9. *You can save on car costs when you keep your eye on the gasoline.* Your car travels about twelve thousand miles a year. You get between eight and twelve miles for a gallon of gasoline. That means you use from a thousand to fifteen hundred gallons a year. Cut your gasoline cost by four cents a gallon—and put an extra forty to sixty dollars in your pocket. Here's how to do it:

- Buy only the octane power you need. All the new cars, no matter what size, run on "regular" octane fuel. So why buy the higher-priced, high-powered variety?
- Shop for the lowest octane your car can use, at the lowest price you can get. With gasoline prices bound to go much higher, a savings of 10 percent or more isn't to be sneezed at.
- Watch your driving habits. A heavy foot on your gas pedal will eat up an extra 10 percent of your

fuel. High speed reduces gas efficiency. So do constant braking and jackrabbit starts.

- Keep your engine properly tuned. That can cut the amount of gas you use by at least 10 percent.

10. *You can save on car costs when you finance your car with a bank loan.* That's the cheapest kind of auto financing you can get. You can pay off in three years at most banks; at some banks in four. If you trade in before three or four years, some plans permit you, after paying twenty-four to thirty-six installments, to pay the rest of the loan in one "balloon payment."

But be careful: If your balloon payment is equal to or less than the trade-in value of the car, you're OK. If your balloon payment is more, you're losing money. The safest procedure is to hold onto the car as long as the car loan lasts and as long as your car holds up.

How much extra money do you have when you finance at a bank? About 5 percent of the purchase price of your car—for every year of the loan!

STEP 2. *Analyze the structure.* There's a general introduction that contains no information you want, so you don't have to study it. There are ten sections, which you'll have to study because each contains information you're looking for.

STEP 3. *Make up a recall pattern.* From your study of the title and the subheads, you recognize that the piece is built around a central idea (how to save dollars) and four subsidiary ideas (how to save dollars on the initial purchase, on trading in, on financing, and on maintenance). These ideas in turn branch out into the specific ideas of

each of the ten sections. To present all these ideas graph-
ically a tree-branch recall pattern would seem to be most
effective. Here's one way it can be set up:

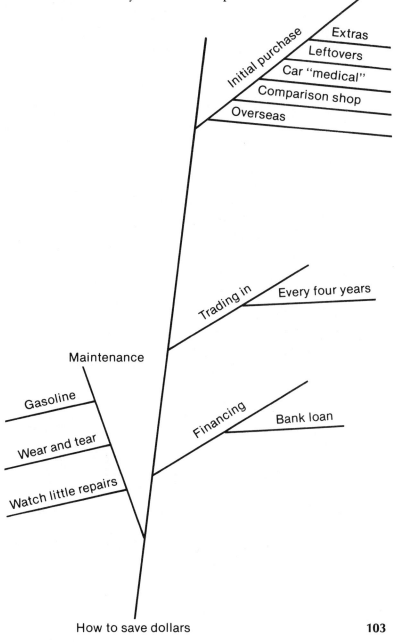

How to save dollars

The recall pattern is well organized. Branching off the right side of the main stem are all the ideas concerning purchasing; branching off on the left side, all ideas concerning maintenance. Organization is the key to an effective recall pattern. (The Who?, Why?, What?, When?, Where?, and How? scheme of organization is not used here because the entire piece answers only one question: How?)

STEP 4. *Review your recall pattern and think about it.* Questions will pop up in your mind. How about octane ratings? Depreciation? Driving habits? Be on the alert for the answers when you take—

STEP 5. *Preview.* Let your brain go quickly but carefully over the material, sorting out related ideas and assessing them in light of your needs and experience.

STEP 6. *Fill in your recall pattern.* Review it and think about it as before. Again, look for the answers to your questions as you take—

STEP 7. *Read dynamically at a speed adjusted to the material.* Most of the material in the tip sheet can be read very rapidly, but you'll have to slow down when you come to the depreciation chart and the arithmetic that follows it.

STEP 8. *Fill in your recall pattern and think about it once again.* Repeated reflection is vital to successful studying. Students who spend a substantial period of their study time thinking about what they've read do much better on tests than students who do not.

STEP 9. *This is the most important step. Recall the information you set out to get.* Do it by talking it out (to somebody else, to yourself, or to a tape recorder). The information is of no use to you under test conditions unless you're able to come up with it easily and rapidly. Recall is practice for test conditions.

Proof that the practice pays off: In one classroom, students spent 20 percent of their study time reading, and 80 percent in recall. In another classroom, the students spent 20 percent of their study time reading, 20 percent rereading, and 60 percent in recall. The students who spent 80 percent in recall did better in tests than the students who spent 60 percent in recall. For study purposes, recall proved superior to rereading.

STEP 10. *Postview each section rapidly and pick up everything you may have missed.* Put the final touches on your recall pattern, and once again recall.

Check Your Study Effectiveness

In real life you better know the difference between a true statement and a false statement concerning car purchasing and maintenance, or it will cost you dollars. You've just studied the subject. Test yourself.

	TRUE	FALSE
1. When you use a car-buying service, your total costs are greater than if you had bought the car by yourself.	☐	☐
2. You can check to see if your repair bills are fair by referring to the *Blue Book*.	☐	☐
3. Buying a car abroad will cost you less than buying the same make and model in the United States.	☐	☐
4. Extras may create extra maintenance problems.	☐	☐

5. Fixing little things that go wrong when they go wrong does not help cut major repair bills. ☐ ☐

6. Trading in your car every four years is preferable to trading it in every two years. ☐ ☐

7. You can get a discount when you buy a leftover. ☐ ☐

8. Jackrabbit starts and sudden stops up the wear and tear on your car, but save gas. ☐ ☐

9. Regular octane is the best buy. ☐ ☐

10. When a balloon payment is more than the trade-in value of your car, you make money. ☐ ☐

Here are the answers: 1. False. 2. False. 3. True. 4. True. 5. False. 6. True. 7. True. 8. False. 9. True. 10. False.

Score ten points for every correct answer.

How did you do?

Ninety? Great!

But go back and postview the section containing the answer to the question you missed.

If you're a student preparing for a classroom test, and you study the same way, chances are your test score will improve substantially. That's why Evelyn Wood campus programs, in which students are drilled in reading and study skills, are flourishing all over the country, from New York University to California Western. (There are also junior rapid reading and college-bound programs. All programs are designed to help young people read effectively, learn more, and become better students.)

Studying from the Spoken Word

You're at a lecture, a seminar, a business meeting. You scribble notes hastily. When you look at them later on, they don't make too much sense to you. Much of what you had to know is gone. Yet you're going to be tested on it in the classroom or in real life. How can you prevent this deficiency from happening again?

The answer is the Evelyn Wood note-taking system.

It's a variation of MRP. Here's how the basic elements of that process—preview, reading, and postview—are adapted to the spoken word:

- *Preview* becomes *prelisten*. You usually have some idea of what you're about to hear. You know the subject of a lecture; you may even have a synopsis of the items to be covered. Seminars often supply printed résumés of the papers to be presented. And what's a business meeting without an agenda? Go over whatever advance information you have, decide what you want to get out of it, then make up a recall pattern. It will guide you through the lecture.
- *Read* becomes *listen*. Following the recall pattern will increase your concentration, and that in turn will improve your comprehension. As you listen, just as when you read, extract the ideas and main points first, then the related details. But don't wait until the session's over to fill in your recall pattern. Do it while you're listening.

- *Postview* becomes *postlisten*. Go over your recall pattern. Include anything you may have failed to put down. Then *recall* by talking about everything you wanted to get out of the lecture. If you're a student, repeat the recall several times before test time. If you're out in the world, and the information is important to you, repeat the recall until you feel you can use the material whenever you need to.

And here's a plus:

You can apply this note-taking system to studying from radio, TV, recordings, computers, and films. You can even use it to scout your next opponent in a tennis tournament.

8

How to Slash Business and Professional Reading Time by Two Thirds or More, Cut Costs, and Increase Efficiency

You're a corporate executive. You receive the following memo. It's from top brass and you must read it at once. But you have to leave for a meeting in about a minute. What do you do?

Use MRP.

MEMO:
To all executive personnel.
FROM:
John White, Executive Vice President,
Manpower Planning
SUBJECT:
Cutting costs while improving productivity with Reading Dynamics

1. PURPOSE OF THIS MEMO
   To acquaint all executive personnel with a new method to get all necessary reading done in the shortest possible time. The method is called Evelyn Wood Reading Dynamics.

2. BACKGROUND BRIEFING

National surveys indicate you spend from
1 hour to 4 hours a day on business reading. Some of you spend as much as 2¾
hours on technical literature, reports,
correspondence, contracts, proposals,
trade journals, newsletters, etc., and 1¼
hours on optional reading to improve
your general competence.

It is estimated that more than 60 million
pages of technical material is printed
each year, and to keep up with developments in your field you are obliged to go
through about 100,000 words a day.

IMPORTANT: You are now averaging 2
hours a day in on-premise reading, which
represents 25 percent of your work time.
In other words, only 75 percent of your
work time is directly productive.

3. THE HIGH COST OF READING

The cost to the company of each executive—including fringe benefits and ex-
penses—averages $50,000 a year. Since
25 percent of your time is spent reading
(and that's a conservative figure), the annual reading cost per executive is
$12,500. There are 20 executives in this
company.

IMPORTANT: We are now paying about $250,000 a year just to have our executives read! Please consider this figure with care.

4. CUTTING READING TIME
An Evelyn Wood Reading Dynamics course for executives in other corporations has increased average reading speed three times.

IMPORTANT: That means your reading time will be cut by about two thirds (or more if you're above average).

5. SAVINGS FROM READING DYNAMICS
Reading Dynamics will cut your reading time from 25 percent of your work time to only 8⅓ percent.

IMPORTANT: The cost of reading time will be cut to $83,300 from $250,000—a savings of $166,700!

The savings will be funded into sales promotion as well as into research and development, which will be conducive to increased corporation profits. A consistent growth pattern will be reflected in your income.

6. RETURN ON INVESTMENT IS HIGH
The cost of the Evelyn Wood course for
20 executives is about $10,000.

IMPORTANT: Since savings amount to
$166,700, the return on our investment
is 1,667 percent! ($166,700 divided by
$10,000).

7. INCREASED PRODUCTIVITY
Speed reading is only one aspect of Reading Dynamics. You will also learn how to
increase comprehension; remember more
longer; take concise, useful notes; organize what you read for more efficient use,
and even write better reports.

IMPORTANT: You will have 16.7 percent
more productive work time, and you will
use that time more productively, since
you will be able to utilize what you read
more effectively. We anticipate that you
will be able to assume new responsibil-
ities and advance your career.

8. CLASS SCHEDULE
Indicate your time preference below. A
class schedule will be set up on the basis
of majority preference.
☐ Luncheon class
☐ Evening class
☐ Saturday morning class

This memo is applicable to professionals and business-persons of all types, as well as to corporate executives. All these people have to read faster, study better, and learn more easily in order to win in the competitive race for success. They also have to get the most from the spoken word, for business and professional life is replete with meetings, conventions, round-table discussions, study groups, lectures, and seminars. In short, they have to learn how to receive information efficiently and to process it effectively. The Evelyn Wood techniques, which you have learned about in this book, help them to do both.

But if you're a professional or a businessperson, you know that success also depends on your ability to communicate the information that has become a part of you. One of the communication areas in which you, like many others, may have experienced some difficulty is report writing. Evelyn Wood principles and techniques can help you take control in that area.

How to Plan a Report

You've absorbed a great deal of information about a subject the Evelyn Wood way, and now you have to write a report on one aspect of the subject. Here's one way you can do it:

1. *Preview.* Go over the material rapidly in your mind. Pick up the main idea for your report. Then add the associated details.

2. *Set up a recall pattern.* That means organizing your material in such a way that it will guide you while writing the report.

3. *Read.* Follow the recall pattern, and read off the pertinent material in your mind. As you do, add it to your recall pattern.

4. *Think about your recall pattern.* Questions will arise in your mind. Look for their answers when you—

5. *Postview.* Go back over the material in your mind and clarify all the questionable points.

6. *Complete your recall pattern.*

7. *Using your recall pattern as a guide, write your report.*

You'll find that your report, built around a central idea with subsidiary ideas and details connected to it in an organized way, will be easy for your audience to understand and hard for them to forget.

You can plan any kind of presentation the same way, including term papers, sales talks, proposals, speeches, memos, even novels. This book was written using those seven simple steps.

Test Your New Business Communications Skills

If you're a professional or a businessperson, chances are you'll come in tomorrow morning to an in-box crammed with correspondence, memos, reports, proposals, sales promotion pieces, trade journals, and all sorts of reading matter you can't afford not to go through.

Go through them—with MRP.

Try a letter. At a glance you'll see what kind of a letter it is, grasp its basic idea, and decide whether it's even worth consideration before you take the time to read it.

Try a memo. You'll pick out the meat in seconds. And if it's important, you'll set up a mental recall pattern so you can bring what you have to know to mind swiftly when you have to use it.

Try a technical journal. You know that summaries are often found in last paragraphs. So you start the article by skipping over to the end. Why waste time plodding from start to finish?

And when it's time to dictate memos and letters, do a mental MRP of the pertinent matter stored in the memory banks of your mind before you utter a word. You'll not only speed up your dictation time, but also the pieces that go out over your signature will be clear, concise, and to the point.

Both your business communication input and output will take you less time. You'll have more time for "action" business and more time to read more. And those are musts for getting ahead.

9

Answers to Your Questions About Evelyn Wood Reading Dynamics

Is this book a résumé of the Evelyn Wood Reading Dynamics course?

No, it's not. It presents the ideas and the main points of the Evelyn Wood system of learning. There are many kinds of Evelyn Wood courses—for general readers, for college students, for college-bound students, for junior readers, and for professionals and businesspeople. The reading material used in instruction is tailored to the needs of the participants (textbooks for students, technical papers for professionals, and so on). Instructors are specially trained for particular courses. All courses provide in-depth instruction and intensive drills and exercises.

Does my reading speed before I enter the course determine how fast I'll read when I finish the course?

Generally, no. Reading is basically a skill, and depends more on your attitude and on practice than on your initial reading speed, or even on your IQ or natural reading aptitude. Even if you consider yourself a good reader now, you could be a better one.

I've heard about machines that pace reading speed. How do they compare with using the hand as a pacer?

These machines can pace you to higher speeds in the classroom, but you can't take them with you. Machines have another drawback. They teach you to read at a fixed speed; but to read for increased comprehension and recall, you have to adjust your speed to the material you're reading. Using your hand as a pacer, you can do that easily. Reading Dynamics uses no machines.

Won't it get boring reading at high speed all the time?

Evelyn Wood was once asked, "Can you really read a novel at fifteen thousand words a minute?"

She answered, "Of course. But who would want to?"

One of the features of Reading Dynamics is flexibility. You can adjust your speed to get what you want from anything you read, so there's no chance of speed-monotony putting you to sleep. Even when you read a novel, you'll vary your speeds—dialogue fastest, descriptive passages more slowly, and introspective passages slowest of all. Yet your overall speed will be high—and you'll be able to finish a novel in one evening.

Do I have to develop a photographic memory to improve my recall?

No. With Reading Dynamics you improve your recall by organizing the material (written or spoken) in a visual pattern built around a central idea to which relevant details are connected. Flashing on the pattern in your mind's eye stimulates your memory.

Recall is not memorization. You're not an actor remembering lines. You're in real life where you have to make what you have to learn a part of you so you can use it when you need it. Reading Dynamics' recall techniques help you do just that.

Is there any proof that a dynamic reader retains more longer than a slow reader?

There is. The slow reader reads for small details, not ideas. He can't see the ideas when he reads word for word. It's like not being able to see the forest for the trees. Without grasping the ideas of a piece, it's difficult to recall what you've read, even after a short period of time. The slow reader forgets 80 percent of what he's read in just twenty-four hours. It has been proved that the dynamic reader, using MRP (the Evelyn Wood Multiple Reading Process), can retain more for sixty-three days than a slow reader can retain for one day.

Does Reading Dynamics work with any kind of technical material?

Yes. Naturally, you can't read a textbook on psycho-surgery as rapidly as you can a suspense yarn, but there's often more information crammed into one page of a scientific text than in a whole novel. Reading technical material dynamically increases the speed of information input, with heightened understanding and recall.

Is reading dynamically the same as skimming?

Not at all. When you skim, you consciously shut out some of the text. You gamble on hitting the highlights—and you lose more times than you win. You seldom get the main idea, and when you do, you miss most of the related details. When you read dynamically you see every word, get the idea, and relate the details to it.

What is area reading?

It's a technique discovered by Evelyn Wood of reading whole blocks of copy at once—many lines of copy rather than single lines. The block of copy—the area—is viewed as a whole, much as you view a picture; and the area reader is able to understand the idea even when the words are seen out of order, as in the following simple example.

Don't read the lines in the example one by one, but look at the whole area fast.

Today is the
of birthday
my brother John.

Didn't you get the idea that "Today is the birthday of my brother John" even though the normal positions of "birthday" and "of" are shifted?

In area reading you move down the page, rather than across the page line by line, aided by several hand movements devised by Evelyn Wood. About area reading, Evelyn Wood wrote:

"As I sweep my eyes down the page, I do not have time to stop and consider each word individually . . . I do not have the time to evaluate them until they become part of the whole idea. I become part of what I'm reading, thinking with the author. I receive from the reading more lasting and vivid impressions."

What good is Reading Dynamics if I can't concentrate on what I read?

Reading Dynamics helps you to concentrate. As your hand moves across and down the page rapidly, you must concentrate to keep up with it. Concentration is made easier for you in another way, too:

For a slow reader the things that occur on the printed page are separated widely in time, so nothing seems to happen, and he loses concentration. But for a fast reader, things come together speedily, and the book flows; interest is heightened, and concentration is obtained with less effort.

My reading has improved since I've been reading this book. Should I continue to use Evelyn Wood techniques?

Yes. Reading dynamically is a skill, and like any skill it requires practice. Tackle all your reading with Evelyn Wood techniques. You can also practice with proven drills under trained instructors in an Evelyn Wood course. Evelyn Wood graduates have the privilege of attending as many tuition-free continuation classes as often as they wish to sharpen their reading skills.

How does Evelyn Wood Reading Dynamics differ from other speed-reading courses?

Reading Dynamics is not just a speed-reading course. What good will it do you to read fast if you don't understand what you read, and can't remember it? Evelyn Wood Reading Dynamics is a revolutionary system of learning. It can be applied not only to printed matter, but also to other visual communication media (TV, film, videotape, computer) as well as to oral communication media (lectures, seminars, meetings, radio, cassettes and so on).

Where are Evelyn Wood Reading Dynamics courses given?

Throughout the world. Check the white pages of your phone book for the Evelyn Wood Reading Dynamics Institute nearest you. Or write to me at Evelyn Wood Reading Dynamics, Inc., 155 Bovet Road, San Mateo, CA

94402. Special on-site classes can be set up for corporations, institutions, chambers of commerce, schools and
colleges, and other organizations even when there is no
Evelyn Wood Reading Dynamics Institute in your region.

Does Reading Dynamics work for everybody?

Only about 3 percent of more than a million Evelyn
Wood graduates failed to triple their skills without loss of
comprehension. No graduate stayed at his or her initial
level of speed/comprehension or dropped lower.

You've been practicing the basics of Reading Dynamics as you read through this book. Is Reading Dynamics
working for *you?* Take this—

Final Test

You opened this book with a purpose in mind: to learn
how to read faster and how to learn better. If you did,
Reading Dynamics *is* working for you. Find out by answering these questions:

	YES	NO
Did you learn—		
How to read without saying the words to yourself?	☐	☐
How to read in groups of words, rather than one word at a time?	☐	☐
How to identify your slow reading habits?	☐	☐
How to break your slow reading habits by replacing them with one fast reading habit?	☐	☐

	YES	NO
How to use your hand as a pacer?	☐	☐
How to break your own reading speed record?	☐	☐
How to improve your comprehension at least one grade?	☐	☐
How to increase your vocabulary without using a dictionary?	☐	☐
How to read with a definite pre-established purpose?	☐	☐
How to pick out the idea from whatever you're reading?	☐	☐
How to organize the ideas and details of what you read into a visual pattern to increase your understanding and recall?	☐	☐
How to boost your recall effectiveness at least one grade?	☐	☐
How to read a book?	☐	☐
How to breeze through news articles and magazine articles?	☐	☐
How to study better, and get 90 percent on an exam?	☐	☐
How to adjust your speed to different kinds of materials to get the most out of them?	☐	☐

	YES	NO
How to take notes that pay off?	☐	☐
How to study from lectures, the TV screen, seminars, and other nonprint media?	☐	☐
How to cut the high costs of on-the-job reading?	☐	☐
How to plan more effective memos, letters, and reports?	☐	☐
How to use a unique Multiple Reading Process (MRP) to get more out of anything you read faster—including technical material?	☐	☐
How to think sharper as you read?	☐	☐
How to open up a world of incomparable wonder and pleasure—the world of books?	☐	☐

More Yes than No answers means that Evelyn Wood Reading Dynamics *is* working for you.

With practice, it will work even better.